Contemporary's

Essentials of Reading

Book 6

Contemporary's
Essentials of
Reading

Book 6

Wright Group

Photo and Art Credits

Cover Daryl Benson/Masterfile; 4, 6 Aaron Haupt; 13 Rudi VonBriel; 24 through 80 Aaron Haupt; 85 Doug Martin; 87 file photo; 88 (burger) Latent Image, (hot dog) Elain Shay; 97 Aaron Haupt.

Permission Acknowledgment

Reprinted with the permission of Atheneum Books for Young Readers, an imprint of Simon & Schuster Children's Publishing Division from A GATHERING OF DAYS by Joan W. Blos. Copyright © 1979 Joan Blos.

Wright Group

ISBN: 0-07-282265-1

Send all inquiries to:
Wright Group/McGraw-Hill
130 E. Randolph, Suite 400
Chicago, IL 60601

Printed in the United States of America.

4 5 6 7 8 9 10 QPD 08 07 06 05

The **McGraw·Hill** Companies

The editorial staff wishes to gratefully acknowledge the contributions of the following advisors, reviewers, and writers, whose considerable efforts, suggestions, ideas, and insights helped to make this text a more valuable and viable learning tool.

Advisory Board for the *McGraw-Hill/Contemporary Essentials of Reading Series*

JoAnn Bukovich-Henderson
Director, Adult Education
SE Regional Resource Center
Juneau, Alaska

Dr. William Walker
Assistant Superintendent
Adult Basic Education
Knox County Schools
Knoxville, Tennessee

Nancy Wilson-Webb
Co-op Director
Adult Basic Education
Fort Worth ISD Consortium
Fort Worth, Texas

Contributing Writers

Jeanne M. Lance
Program Coordinator
Ohio Family Literacy Statewide Initiative
Ohio Department of Education
Columbus, Ohio

Dr. Nancy Burkhalter
Language and Literacy Consultant
Laramie, Wyoming

Dr. Nora Ruth Roberts
Composition and Literature Instructor
Hunter College — Medgar Evers
   Affiliate of CUNY
New York, New York

Elizabeth Shupe
ABE/ESL Instructor
Right to Read of Weld County
Greeley, Colorado

Dea McAuliffe
Buffalo City Public Schools
Buffalo, New York

Patricia Costello
ABE/ESL Instructor
San Francisco City College
San Francisco, California

Clarita D. Henderson
Educational Consultant
Buffalo, New York

Rita Milios
Toledo, Ohio

Laura Belgrave
Largo, Florida

Doug Hutzelman
Kettering, Ohio

Christina Hutzelman
Kettering, Ohio

Reviewers

Connie J. Dodd
ABE Instructor
Frontier Central School District
Hamburg, New York

Julie Gerson
Coordinator
Goodwill Literary Institute
Pittsburgh, Pennsylvania

Linda Lockhart
ABE/GED Instructor
Pines Plaza GED
Pembroke Pines, Florida

Rubianna M. Porter
Director of Precollege Programs
Cleveland State Community College
Cleveland, Tennessee

Laura Weidner, Director
Applied Technology and
   Apprenticeship
Catonsville Community College
Catonsville, Maryland

Linda J. McGuire
Coordinator
Adult Learning Center
Lawrence Public Schools
Lawrence, Kansas

Christine M. Johnson
ABE/GED Instructor
Adult Learning Center
Lawrence Public Schools
Lawrence, Kansas

Table of Contents

Nutrition, Health, and Safety

Workplace Skills

The Reading Corner

Name _____ Pretest for Book 6

A. Put a √ next to the synonym for the first word.

1. wealthy a. _____ rich   b. _____ poor

2. old   a. _____ young   b. _____ ancient

B. Put a √ next to the antonym for the first word.

3. dislike   a. _____ hate   b. _____ like

4. apart   a. _____ together   b. _____ far away

C. Put a √ next to the word with the stronger feeling or meaning in each row.

5. a. _____ bad   b. _____ horrible

6. a. _____ looking   b. _____ staring

7. a. _____ shouted   b. _____ called

D. Put a √ next to the word that has a **k sound** for the letters **ch.**

8. a. _____ achieve   b. _____ chorus

9. a. _____ chilly   b. _____ echo

10. a. _____ anchor   b. _____ chicken

E. Put a √ next to the two words in each row that have the same long vowel sound.

11. a. _____ coach   b. _____ motel   c. _____ coward

12. a. _____ rope   b. _____ touch   c. _____ soak

F. Make the following words show ownership.

13. the house that belongs to the aunt

_____

14. the toys that belong to the boys

_____

G. Put a √ next to the meaning of the underlined word.

15. The water pipe <u>burst</u> last night.

a. _____ broke   b. _____ rushed in

16. I am going to the <u>hearing</u> this afternoon.

a. _____ listening   b. _____ court case

H. Read the story. Put a √ next to the best answer.

I was young and out of a job. I became very worried. A friend suggested that I look into becoming a piano tuner. I thought she was kidding. "I don't have perfect pitch," I said. I could never hum a music note without help.

Besides, I didn't know where you go to study to be a piano tuner. I called several people. They told me I didn't need perfect pitch. I only needed normal hearing. I knew I could hear OK. So I decided to give it a try.

I found two ways to get training. I could go to a piano-tuning school, or I could become an apprentice. An apprentice is someone who learns a trade from a master. The master is already in the trade. He or she knows the job very well and teaches others.

I decided to find a master piano tuner to teach me.

17. What was the story mostly about?

    a. _____ Learning to play the piano

    b. _____ Being without a job

    c. _____ Finding out how to become a piano tuner

18. An apprentice is someone who

    a. _____ knows how to play the piano.

    b. _____ is studying a trade from a master.

    c. _____ is unemployed.

19. Perfect pitch means

    a. _____ a person can throw a baseball.

    b. _____ a person knows the words to most songs.

    c. _____ a person can hum a note without help.

20. A person can become a piano tuner by

    a. _____ learning to play the piano.

    b. _____ working as an apprentice and going to piano-tuning school.

    c. _____ working as an apprentice or going to piano-tuning school.

Grandma Moves In

FAMILY LIFE

Read about a family facing change.

A Bad Fall

Verona Dombrick was 78 years old when she fell and broke her hip. Mrs. Dombrick's daughter, Margo, got a call from the hospital soon after the accident. She dressed quickly and rushed over, leaving her husband with their two sons. A doctor told Margo that her mother would need an operation. Then she would need treatment in a skilled care **facility** for a few weeks. Her hip would be repaired, but it would never be the same.

"I'm afraid your mother can't live on her own for a long time," the doctor said **grimly.** "It will take her months to walk properly again. At first, she'll have to use a walker. She'll probably feel weak and out of sorts."

"My children love their grandma. We all do. We'll make room for her at my house." Margo bit down on her lip, trying not to cry. "Poor Mother. My father died 15 years ago, and she has lived on her own since then. Giving up her independence will not be easy."

"Change never is," the doctor said softly.

facility *a building used for some activity or service*

grimly *unsmilingly*

Getting Ready for Grandma

That night, Margo and her husband, Allan, had a long talk about the situation. Together they decided that Mrs. Dombrick would come to live with them.

In the following days, the family worked hard to prepare their home for Mrs. Dombrick's stay. Micah, the younger son, gave up his room so Grandma Dombrick could have it for **privacy.** He moved in with his brother, Christopher. Christopher's room was larger than Micah's, but it wasn't big and the boys were **cramped.**

privacy *a place or situation in which a person is out of public view*

cramped *close and crowded*

Allan painted Micah's old room. He wanted it to be fresh and welcoming for his mother-in-law. The doctor gave Allan a booklet to help him make the house safer for her. He went around the house and removed all the throw rugs so she wouldn't fall. Later, he mounted a grab bar on the bathtub and put nonskid tape inside the tub.

Margo also read the booklet. She then made sure there were night-lights in every room. She rearranged furniture to free up space.

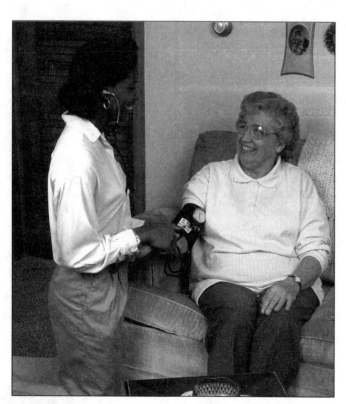

During spare moments, she made telephone calls to find out what her mother would need. She found out that her mother could get home health care while she recovered. Medicare would help pay some of the costs for home health care workers.

Medicare is a government health program for the elderly. The health care workers would help Mrs. Dombrick bathe, take her blood pressure, and help in ways that family members could not.

Knowing there was help available eased Margo's mind. Neither she nor Allan could just quit their jobs or afford to take time off.

A Challenge Every Day

Finally, Mrs. Dombrick was allowed to leave the skilled care facility. She appeared smaller and weaker to Margo, like a winter tree without its leaves. Margo didn't say anything, though. She carefully drove her mother home. Then she got her settled in a chair.

The boys stood around with their hands in their pockets. They smiled, but they weren't sure what to say or do.

Grandma Dombrick looked at them and smiled back. "Thank you for sharing a room so that I could have my own," she said in a tiny voice. "I hope it isn't too much of a problem."

"Oh no, Grandma," the boys hurried to say. "It's no big deal."

But it was, and so were other things. As the weeks went by, the boys began to **bicker** and complain that Grandma Dombrick took too long in the bathroom. At night, Allan sighed when his mother-in-law listened to her radio.

bicker *fight and quarrel*

"She plays it so loud," he said to Margo one night.

"I know," Margo answered. "Her hearing isn't what it used to be. I can't believe I never noticed before."

There were other hardships, too. The health care workers didn't arrive first thing in the morning, and they weren't there at night. Margo had to help her mother get dressed and undressed. She had to help her in the bathroom and see that she took her medicine. It seemed as if one or the other of them was dashing to the store 10 times a day for things her mother needed.

Now and then, Margo needed to check on her mother's house to be certain it was OK during her mother's **absence**. And although the walker helped Mrs. Dombrick move around, it tired her out. At times, she got cranky.

absence *time away from a place or an event*

Every day was a challenge. Sometimes, Margo wondered if they would all make it.

Tears and Laughter

One evening Christopher waved his report card and proudly announced, "Look, everyone, I got an 'A' in history!"

"That's great!" said Margo. She reached for a hug, but Christopher was already headed toward his grandma. Margo watched her son **embrace** the old woman.

embrace *to hug*

"Thanks for all your help, Grandma," Christopher said.

Mrs. Dombrick laughed. "History I know," she said. "I've lived a long time."

It suddenly struck Margo that she had not paid attention to the positive things that her mother had brought into the home. She had not noticed her mother helping Christopher with homework. She had **overlooked** how often the boys played board games with her instead of watching TV. She had forgotten how much her mother helped with dinner.

overlooked
ignored or not noticed something

Margo was surprised to feel a tear slide down her cheek. She wiped it away and smiled. She didn't wonder if they would make it anymore. They were making it, day by day. And that was fine. That was family.

McGraw-Hill/Contemporary Essentials of Reading   Book 6

Words, Words, Words

A. A **prefix** is a group of letters that are used to begin some words. The prefix **pre-** means before something in place or time. The prefix **pro-** means forward or to be in favor of something. For example:

The *pre*dawn temperature felt muggy.
  The temperature before dawn was muggy.

The man was *pro*-American all the way.
  The man favored American things all the way.

Rocket fuel would *pro*pel the shuttle from Earth.
  Rocket fuel would push the shuttle forward from Earth.

Read the sentences below. Each sentence has an underlined word with the prefix **pre-** or **pro-**. Explain what each sentence means. Use the examples above to help you.

1. The woman bought a <u>preshrunk</u> blouse.

   _____

2. The teacher wanted to <u>promote</u> her students.

   _____

3. Margo had to <u>preheat</u> the oven before putting in the roast.

   _____

4. Republicans and Democrats are <u>pro-democracy.</u>

   _____

5. The businessman had to <u>prepay</u> for his plane ticket.

   _____

Word Story:

Want ads *are usually found in newspapers. They list information about jobs that are available.*

B. Writers use words that give strong feelings. These words help you understand and enjoy the story. **Connotation** is a word that asks you what *feeling* the words in a story have. For example:

1. The wind blew against the door.

2. The cold, frosty wind hit hard against the door.

Which sentence gives you a stronger feeling? Did you say sentence 2? Read the sentences below. Circle the words that give you a strong feeling. The first one is done for you.

1. The kitchen had a (strong) (sickening) odor of garlic.

2. David threw the ball across a field of thin, dry grass.

3. The huge, dangerous lion roared mightily.

4. The mirror was smashed into a thousand tiny, sharp pieces.

5. Cheryl tried hard to comfort the crying, red-faced baby.

C. When two vowels are together, they sometimes have one sound. For example, the vowels **oa** together have the long vowel sound of **o.** Words such as *soap, roast, grow,* and *toe* have the long vowel sound of **o.** Put a √ next to the two words in each row that have the same long vowel sound. The first one is done for you.

1. a. __√__ coach   b. __√__ motel   c. _____ coward

2. a. _____ frozen   b. _____ slop   c. _____ cocoa

3. a. _____ envelope   b. _____ loan   c. _____ jolly

4. a. _____ touch   b. _____ slope   c. _____ soak

5. a. _____ blower   b. _____ floppy   c. _____ throat

D. The consonants **sh** can give the sound you hear in **sh**ower or **sh**oulder. Use **sh** to complete the missing words. The first one is done for you.

1. The man had to __sh__ave his face twice a day.

2. The noon sun cast a long _____adow on the lawn.

3. You _____ould _____ield your eyes from the sun.

4. The _____irtless boy stood _____yly to the side.

5. "_____uffle the cards," the man said _____arply.

Understanding

A. A **fact** is something you know is true from the story. An **opinion** is something you feel or believe about the story. Use the story to decide if the statements below are facts or opinions. Write **F** for a fact or **O** for an opinion. The first two are done for you.

1. __F__ Grandma Dombrick is 78 years old.

2. __O__ Grandma Dombrick is too old to live alone.

3. _____ Margo and Allan both have jobs.

4. _____ Allan reads a booklet the doctor gave him.

5. _____ Christopher gets an "A" in history on his report card.

6. _____ Grandma Dombrick plays her radio loudly.

7. _____ Loud radios have made Grandma Dombrick hard of hearing.

B. Answer the questions below. Give reasons for your answers.

1. Do you think Grandma Dombrick will want to move back into her own home after her hip is healed? _____

   _____

2. In what ways do you think Grandma Dombrick's life might be different after she is better? _____

   _____

3. Do you think Micah and Christopher were happy to have their grandmother living with them? _____

   _____

4. Do you think Christopher will still do well with his schoolwork if his grandmother moves out? _____

   _____

Discussion

A. Use the story to help you answer the questions below.

1. List three things that Margo's husband, Allan, did to get their house ready for Grandma Dombrick's visit.

   a. _____

   b. _____

   c. _____

2. List three facts from the story about Grandma Dombrick.

   a. _____

   b. _____

   c. _____

B. Answer the questions below. Use the story to help you.

1. Why couldn't Grandma Dombrick live alone anymore?

   _____

2. Why were Micah and Christopher bickering with each other?

   _____

3. Who helped Christopher with his history test?

   _____

4. Write two good things that happened because Grandma Dombrick moved in with her daughter's family.

   _____

   _____

Becoming a Citizen

Read how Neda becomes a U.S. citizen.

An Important Letter

Neda Kolich climbed the steep steps to the apartment she rented on the top floor. "Another long day," she sighed, glad to be home. All her muscles ached from scrubbing floors at the business tower where she worked.

Neda removed the mail from her mailbox and unlocked her apartment door. "A cup of tea will feel good right now," she thought. After Neda started the kettle, she sat down at her small kitchen table. As she looked through the mail, she saw an official-looking letter. "Could this be it?" she asked herself. She looked at the return address. It was from the Office of Immigration and Naturalization Service.

Neda had applied for U.S. citizenship six months earlier. She had filled out the N-400 Form with all its personal questions. Some of the questions **pertained** to her marital status and the number of children she had. She answered "divorced" to the first one and "1 child" to the other question. Ages and names were also **required.** She had filled in her son's name and age: Igor Kolich, Age 18. Neda had answered all the questions. She had even provided an official card with her fingerprints for an FBI background check.

pertained *related to*

required *needed*

Neda opened the envelope. The letter said:

> Please appear at 321 Fourth Street, Room C,
> on June 16 at 9:30 A.M. for your **hearing.**

hearing *a legal interview*

Paperwork

Neda stared at the letter for a few minutes. So this was it. After all the paperwork, the $95.00 fee, the photographs and fingerprints, the day had finally arrived. Neda was used to filing papers and waiting for services. It had taken quite a while to get the papers allowing her and her son to come to the U.S.

She and her son, Igor, had come together. When they arrived in the port at New York, they went through a government agency to find housing. In the beginning, they lived in a low-income housing **project.** Neda's new apartment was much nicer. The neighborhood was safe, and she liked her landlady, Mrs. Forello. Mrs. Forello had even helped her a little with the citizenship forms.

project *apartment buildings or houses*

There had been so many papers in the beginning. There were medical forms and papers to open the gas and electric accounts. And, of course, there was Igor's application to college and his **scholarship.**

scholarship *a grant of money for schooling*

interrupted *stopped*

The kettle whistled and **interrupted** her thoughts. Neda poured herself a cup of tea. As she quietly sipped her tea, she thought about the past six years. There had been some difficult times, but now everything seemed to be working out.

Preparing for the Interview

The next day was Neda's day off from work. She usually did her shopping at the local open market. People from many countries ran the market stands. Neda had gotten to know many of them. Some of them were from her hometown, Zagreb, in Croatia. She hadn't known them there, but they had become friends since meeting at the market.

At the market, Neda met her friend, Maya. She told her about the letter from the INS.

"Finally!" Maya exclaimed. "Well, I hope things go better for you than they did for my father-in-law. He filed too early—four years and eight months to be **exact.** He should have waited another month, but he was worried about losing his benefits. He is on **disability,** you know."

exact *just right*

disability *physical problem*

Neda nodded **sympathetically.** She was glad that she and Igor were in good health.

sympathetically *with understanding for another's feelings*

Time to Review

When Neda got home, she thought about her upcoming interview on June 16. Her English was pretty good, so that didn't worry her. She hoped she remembered her American history and government. The INS office had given her a list of questions. She had been studying for the past six months. The test was in two weeks. "It's time to review," she thought. Neda got the list of questions and began reading.

- Who was the first President? "That was easy," she thought — "George Washington."
- How many branches of government are there? "Three."

Neda continued down the list. She knew almost all the answers. She had a hard time remembering the name of her U.S. Representative. Her name was difficult to **pronounce.** Neda knew that a correct answer was important. She thought, "I guess I had better study this a little more. Two weeks can pass very quickly."

pronounce *to say*

The Citizenship Interview

Neda arrived at the INS office early on June 16 and went directly to Room C. She put her letter in a box and took a seat in the waiting room. Around 10:15, a young clerk called her name, "Neda Kolich." Neda followed him into a private office where she met the INS officer, Ms. Allen.

"Raise your right hand," the INS officer instructed. Neda did as the woman asked and listened carefully.

swear *to promise*

"Do you **swear** to tell the truth?" the woman asked.

"Yes," Neda answered.

"I am going to ask you to write a sentence for me in English," Ms. Allen said.

Neda wrote slowly and handed the paper to Ms. Allen. The officer looked at it and said, "That's fine. Now I want to ask you a few questions about the U.S. government."

Citizenship Questions

Ms. Allen asked Neda, "How many senators are there in Congress?"

Neda answered correctly with, "One hundred. Two from each state."

"Who is your representative in the House of Representatives?" Neda also answered this correctly.

Ms. Allen asked several other questions, and Neda knew these answers, too. Then, she asked Neda questions about her personal history. These questions were meant to **verify** the answers Neda had given on her original application.

verify *to prove something is true*

Finally, Ms. Allen asked, "Why do you want to become an American citizen?"

Neda thought about many answers and gave the best answer she could think of. "I want to vote. "

Ms. Allen asked Neda to sign her name next to her picture. "Congratulations! You passed and will receive a notice about the swearing-in ceremony."

Neda shook hands with Ms. Allen and thanked her. Neda was very happy and wanted to tell the good news to her son and friends.

Words, Words, Words

A. **Synonyms** are words that have the same or similar meanings. Match the words below with their underlined synonyms in the sentences. The first one is done for you.

ached   kettle   scrubbing   applied   verify
pronounce   several   swear   nervous

1. Tessa was <u>anxious</u> about her answers. _____**nervous**_____

2. His muscles <u>hurt</u> after lifting heavy boxes all day. _____

3. The little girl tried to <u>say</u> the long name. _____

4. Igor was <u>rubbing</u> the stain from the rug. _____

5. She put the <u>teapot</u> on the stove. _____

6. David also <u>filed</u> for U.S. citizenship. _____

7. The officer tried to <u>check</u> that her answers were true. _____

8. Soheil will <u>promise</u> to tell the truth. _____

9. Helen had <u>many</u> friends at the market. _____

B. Some words have more than one meaning. Read the sentences below. Put a √ next to the word that has the same meaning as the underlined word in the sentence.

1. Olga will go with you to the <u>hearing</u> on Wednesday.

   a. _____ ability to hear   b. _____ official meeting

2. David has an apartment in the new downtown <u>project</u>.

   a. _____ building   b. _____ assignment

3. Joyce goes to the <u>market</u> every Saturday.

    a. _____ to sell   b. _____ a place to shop

4. The INS officer asked, "Do you <u>swear</u> to tell the truth?"

    a. _____ make a promise   b. _____ use profanity

5. "Raise your right hand," the INS officer <u>instructed.</u>

    a. _____ taught   b. _____ gave an order or
                                                   direction

C. The word *know* begins with the two consonants **kn.** When you say the word *know,* you hear the *n* but not the *k.* Write a sentence for the following **kn** words.

1. knew _____

2. knot _____

3. knee _____

4. knit _____

D. **Compound** words are two words that are written together to make a new word. For example: *fingerprint* is a compound word made up of the word *finger* and the word *print.* Read the words below. Put a √ next to the compound words. Then, write a sentence for them.

1. _____ apartment   2. _____ herself   3. _____ textbook

4. _____ slowly   5. _____ sidewalk   6. _____ teapot

7. _____ instructed   8. _____ landlady   9. _____ hearing

10. _____

11. _____

12. _____

13. _____

14. _____

Understanding

Read the questions below. Use your own ideas to answer them.

1. Now that Neda is a citizen, how will her life change?

_____

_____

_____

2. What do you think would have happened if Neda had not passed the citizenship test?

_____

_____

_____

3. Ms. Allen asked Neda why she wanted to be a citizen. Do you think Neda gave a good answer? Explain your answer.

_____

_____

4. Why do you think it took so long for Neda to get an answer to her application?

_____

_____

_____

_____

Discussion

A. Read the sentences below. They tell how Neda began her steps to become a citizen. Put the sentences in the order that things happened in the story. The first one is done for you.

a. _____ Neda swears to tell the truth.

b. _____ Neda passes the citizenship test.

c. __1__ Neda receives an official letter.

d. _____ Neda reviews her list of questions.

e. _____ Neda answers Ms. Allen's questions.

f. _____ Neda opens the official letter.

g. _____ Neda goes to the INS office on June 16.

B. Read the questions below. Use the story to help you with your answers.

1. Where did Neda work? _____

2. What form did Neda fill out for citizenship? _____

3. Where did Neda have to appear for her hearing? _____

4. How many children did Neda have? _____

5. How old was Igor? _____

6. Who was Neda's landlady? _____

7. Who instructed Neda to raise her right hand? _____

8. What did Neda answer when she was asked why she wanted to be a citizen? _____

9. Who did Neda want to tell about passing the citizenship test?

_____

A Closer Look at *Test Taking*

When Neda Kolich took the test for U.S. citizenship, she answered many questions about her personal history. She also answered other types of questions. Some were about U.S. history and government. To get ready for the citizenship test, Neda followed some important steps. She started her review early. Whether you are taking a test for citizenship or a reading test for night class or the GED, here are some suggestions for test taking.

Test Taking Tips

1. Prepare early. Don't wait until the day or night before to review your notes and class material.

2. Try to make the test material match things you know in your own life. Rewrite your class notes and put in examples of things you know about.

3. Use memory helps like rhymes or lists or maps.

4. Read your notes out loud whenever possible.

5. Study with someone else. Do this only after you have studied and reviewed well by yourself.

Test Worry

You may still be worried, or scared, about taking a test. Neda knew how important her citizenship test was and how

important it was to do well. Do you think she was nervous or scared? If she was, she didn't appear to be when she took the test. Perhaps she followed some of the following suggestions for dealing with test worry.

1. **Be Prepared.** Being prepared builds your confidence.

2. **Practice.** Make up test questions and answer them. Time yourself while you take a practice test.

3. **Study Groups.** Meet with one or two classmates to review.

4. **Exercise.** Do some type of exercise to reduce stress or worry. Walking, jogging, or stretching exercises can help you.

5. **Before the Test Day.** Ready yourself the night before the test. Lay out your clothes, books, and even your house or car keys. Get a good night's sleep. Set your alarm. Eat a light breakfast. Go over your notes and get to the test with time to spare.

6. **Positive Thinking.** Before you begin the test, take deep breaths and **relax**. You're prepared. Tell yourself, "I can do this."

Question Types

There are different types of tests. Some are true/false, matching, fill-in-the-blank, essay, and multiple choice. The written test for citizenship is a multiple-choice test. There are 20 questions on the test along with a dictation part. Here are some hints about multiple-choice tests.

1. Always read the directions carefully.

2. Make sure you answer all the questions.

3. Do the questions you know first.

4. Use the **process of elimination** when choosing your answer. The process of elimination means that you read through all the answer choices and get rid of the choices you know are incorrect.

Write in your own words how you get ready to take a test.

_____

_____

_____

Taking Time for Your Children

FAMILY LIFE

Meet Gregory Quinn. Read how he learns to make time for his child.

The Family

Elizabeth Quinn was not happy because her husband, Gregory, did not seem to have time for their little girl. He would always say he was too busy. Their daughter, Carly, wanted to play and spend more time with her father. She needed more **attention** from him, but Gregory **seldom** paid attention to her. He **rarely** played games with her, and they didn't talk too much to each other.

Gregory was never mean to Carly. He never yelled at her nor did he ever hit her. Sometimes it seemed as if he just **ignored** her. He never noticed the sad look on the child's face when he made no time for her.

Elizabeth knew things were not right, so she decided to talk to her husband.

attention *notice*

seldom *only once in a while*

rarely *not often*

ignored *failed to notice*

Gregory Explains

"Why don't you ever play games with Carly?" she asked Gregory one evening. "Why don't you talk with her? She is only four years old. She's a little girl, and she needs her father to pay attention to her."

Elizabeth knew it was important for parents to show an interest in their children and to listen to them. She wanted her daughter to grow up with a father who enjoyed being with her.

defensive
protective

"You know how busy I am," Gregory said in a **defensive** voice. "I work all day at the lumber yard, and I do jobs around the house when I am at home. Some evenings I have to go to meetings, and on the weekends I need some time to relax. That's why I go hunting and fishing whenever I have some free time."

"But Carly thinks you don't care about her. She thinks you don't love her," Elizabeth said with tears in her eyes.

"That's not true. You know I love Carly. I work hard to pay for her clothes. She has a lot of toys, and she has you. You are a wonderful mother the way you take such great care of her. She has everything she needs."

"But she needs her daddy, too. She needs you to show your love and interest. You need to talk with her. You could ask her about things, read to her, or play games with her. There are lots of things you two could do together."

Gregory looked down at his hands and then back into his wife's worried eyes. He sighed and said, "OK, I'll try, but I don't know how to play with little girls. I feel silly and that's the truth. I don't like games or tea parties, and I don't care for fairy tales. And I really hate dolls. I love hunting and fishing, and little girls aren't interested in doing those things."

A Good Idea

awkward
uncomfortable

Elizabeth was still unhappy, but she knew Gregory really loved Carly. He felt **awkward** with their child, and Elizabeth felt sorry for him. She gave the problem a lot of thought and finally came up with an idea. "It's true that some little girls aren't interested in hunting, but they love animals and fish," she thought to herself.

The very next afternoon Elizabeth took Carly to the library to look for books about animals and fish. They found some books with big, colorful pictures. Elizabeth and Carly checked out six **oversized** books.

oversized *bigger than most*

After dinner that night, Gregory sat in his chair in the living room reading the evening newspaper. Soon, he noticed Carly sitting quietly on the sofa with two library books.

"Those books look interesting," Gregory said as he put the newspaper down. He got up and went to sit next to Carly. He took one of the oversized books and pointed to a picture of a wild turkey.

"Turkeys live near our town," he started to explain to his daughter. "So do foxes, and they look just like the one in this picture." Gregory pointed to another picture of a red fox. "I saw a fox just like this one when I was in the forest last week."

Answers to Share

Soon Carly climbed onto her father's lap. As Gregory balanced both his daughter and the book, he told her about the animals pictured on the pages. Carly had many questions. She asked about the foxes, the hawks, and the owls. She wanted to know where they slept and what they ate. She asked about the kinds of fish in the nearby streams.

Gregory knew all the answers to Carly's questions, and he happily shared his knowledge with her. Together they turned the pages. Carly happily **chatted** with her father or **contentedly** listened when he read to her from the book. They talked and read together until Carly's bedtime.

chatted *talked happily*

contentedly *felt happy*

The Idea Works

Elizabeth smiled as she watched her husband and their daughter together. She was so happy that her idea seemed to be working. Her husband seemed so relaxed and comfortable with Carly.

interrupt *to stop*

"I hate to **interrupt** you two, but it's time to get ready for bed," Elizabeth said to her sleepy-eyed daughter.

Gregory smiled at his wife and looked down at Carly. "Mommy's right, it's time for bed. We'll read more tomorrow, and this weekend I'll take you to the library for more books."

delighted *very happy*

Carly was **delighted** and asked her father, "Will you take me fishing with you some day, Daddy?"

"I sure will," answered Gregory, "and maybe we'll even take Mommy."

Carly went to get her pajamas, and her parents soon heard her singing. Gregory looked at his wife and put an arm around her shoulder. "I guess I can talk to little girls after all." Then he laughed, "But I still don't think tea parties will ever be my favorite thing to do."

Words, Words, Words

A. **Antonyms** are words that have the opposite meaning. For example, *hot* is the antonym for *cold*. Put a √ next to the antonym for the first word in each line.

1. bored   a. _____ friendly   b. _____ interested   c. _____ quiet

2. smiled   a. _____ frowned   b. _____ cheered   c. _____ looked

3. noisy   a. _____ soft   b. _____ quiet   c. _____ loud

4. small   a. _____ tiny   b. _____ little   c. _____ big

B. **Synonyms** are words that have the same or near the same meanings. For example, *big* is a synonym for *large*. Put a √ next to the synonym for the first word in each line.

1. happy   a. _____ sad   b. _____ joyful   c. _____ unhappy

2. attention   a. _____ care   b. _____ interested   c. _____ ignored

3. seldom   a. _____ often   b. _____ rarely   c. _____ many times

4. awake   a. _____ asleep   b. _____ tired   c. _____ alert

C. **Possessive** words show who or what owns something. You can write many possessive words by adding **'s** or **s'** to the end of the word. For example:

The boy's voice is changing.

The **'s** tells you the changing voice belongs to the boy.

The boys' hats were stolen.

The **s'** tells you the stolen hats belong to more than one boy.

Word Story:

The word asset *means a valuable item that is owned by a business or a person. Some assets are a house, a building, cash, a car, or stock.*

Show ownership in the following sentences by adding **'s** or **s'** to the underlined words. The first two are done for you.

1. <u>Carly</u> book is about animals. _____ **Carly's** _____

2. They looked at many <u>book</u> pictures. _____ **books'** _____

3. A mouse was in the <u>hawk</u> beak. _____

4. Gregory heard two wild <u>turkey</u> voices at once. _____

5. The red <u>fox</u> den is under the roots. _____

6. His <u>father</u> name is Stephen. _____

7. The <u>girl</u> teams meet every other month. _____

D. The letter **y** can sometimes have the **long e** vowel sound as in the word *very*. Complete each sentence with a **long e** word. Write your answer on the line. The first one is done for you.

1. It is wise to (study, apply) before a math test. _____ **study** _____

2. The torn old photo looked (ugly, dry). _____

3. Sue Lee has a very nice (butterfly, family). _____

4. Do you have (my, any) stamps? _____

5. Her first name is (Lucy, Skye). _____

E. The letters **squ** sometimes have the sound of **skw** as in the word *squeeze*. Complete each sentence with one of the **sqw** words below. Make sure your answer fits the meaning of the sentence. Write your answer on the line.

squirm   squash   squeal   squeeze   squint

1. On sunny days, I _____ my eyes a bit.

2. She likes to _____ fresh oranges for morning juice.

3. The little boy tried to _____ the bug.

4. He heard the wild pig _____ before he saw it.

5. The dog tried to _____ under the white fence.

Understanding

A. Answer the questions below. Use the story and your own ideas to give each answer.

1. In the beginning of the story, what was different about Carly's mother and father when they were with her?

_____

2. At the end of the story, what was the same about Carly's mother and father when they were with her?

_____

B. Read the sentences below. Give the best ending for them. Put a √ next to your answer.

1. Carly hoped her father would

    a._____ hunt for foxes.

    b._____ spend time with her.

    c._____ buy her a new doll.

2. Elizabeth knew that her husband felt

    a._____ excited about meetings.

    b._____ unhappy with his job.

    c._____ awkward with Carly.

3. Gregory and Carly will now

    a._____ stop going to the library.

    b._____ enjoy doing things together.

    c._____ go fishing every day of the week.

Discussion

A. Read the sentences below. Show the order in which things happened.

    a. _____ Elizabeth took Carly to the library.

    b. _____ Elizabeth noticed a problem between her husband and her daughter.

    c. _____ Gregory enjoyed reading the animal books with Carly.

    d. _____ Elizabeth checked out six books from the library.

B. A **cause** makes something happen. Read the sentences below. Write the cause on the **Cause** line. Write the effect on the **Effect** line. The first one is done for you.

    1. The big dog barked so the children ran away.

        Cause: the big dog barked _____

        Effect: the children ran away _____

    2. After it rained, the flowers grew tall and straight.

        Cause: _____

        Effect: _____

    3. Mary felt warmer when she put on her jacket.

        Cause: _____

        Effect: _____

    4. Jack broke his leg when he fell off the ladder.

        Cause: _____

        Effect: _____

LESSON 4

Wearing Glasses!

FAMILY LIFE

Read about Elisa Vacarro. She needs glasses, but she is 100 percent against wearing them.

A Worry

Joan Vacarro looked at her 11-year-old daughter as she watched her favorite program on television. She thought Elisa was sitting much too close to the TV. Every evening for the past few weeks she had told Elisa to move back from the TV. She wondered if Elisa needed glasses.

One night after Elisa had gone to bed, Joan talked to her husband about her concerns. She told him that Elisa showed many signs of needing glasses. She sat too close to the TV, and she **squinted** when she looked at something far away. She rubbed her eyes a lot and **complained** of having headaches. She also told him that every time she mentioned the **possibility** of glasses to their daughter, Elisa became very upset. They decided to first check with Elisa's teacher.

A Talk With the Teacher

Joan called Mr. Turner and found out that there were problems at school, too. He had moved Elisa's seat closer to the board, but she still seemed to squint when copying from the

squinted *closed one's eyes part way*

complained *found fault*

possibility *can be done*

board. However, there didn't seem to be a problem with close work at her desk.

Mr. Turner told Joan that he would arrange for the school nurse to give Elisa an eye test. If she failed the school eye test, she would have to see an eye doctor for a complete examination. As they finished their talk, Joan said, "I hope Elisa passes the test. She doesn't want to wear glasses. When I mention them to her, she becomes very upset."

image *a mental idea or picture you have of yourself*

"Sixth graders are very concerned about how they look. Glasses don't fit the **image** of who they want to be," replied Mr. Turner.

Test Results

Later that week, Elisa burst through the kitchen door. "The nurse says I have to go to an eye doctor. I will not wear glasses!"

"Elisa, let's see what the doctor says," her father said.

"Yes," her mother answered calmly. "We will go to the eye doctor and find out what she thinks. OK?"

"I guess so," Elisa answered with tears in her eyes.

"Don't cry, sweetheart," Joan hugged her daughter comfortingly, "and don't worry. We'll do this together."

At the Eye Doctor's Office

optometrist *a person who tests the eyes for vision disorders*

Elisa had a complete eye exam at the **optometrist's** office.

When Gail Lund, the optometrist, entered the examination room, she told Joan and Miguel that Elisa needed glasses. Elisa was nearsighted. She could see well close up but not far away. Dr. Lund wrote Elisa's prescription for glasses and gave it to them to be filled.

Elisa Tells Her Friends

reactions *responses*

Elisa was ready for her best friends' **reactions** when she told them she had to wear glasses.

"Oh, gosh! I don't believe you need glasses!" said Amy.

"I told Mom and Dad that I won't wear them! Everyone will call me a 'four-eyed geek' and make fun of me! I won't have any friends!"

"Sherita and I will still be your friends. You're still the same person. You'll just have glasses. That's all," Amy assured Elisa.

"That's all!" Elisa shouted. "It's the end of the world!"

Amy and Sherita talked about Elisa's problem. They felt sorry for her because they knew that their classmates weren't always kind.

Getting Glasses

Joan checked out many opticians before she chose *Glasses by Paul Leff*. Friends had told her that Paul Leff had frames in many styles and price ranges. Joan hoped there would be frames Elisa would like and would wear. As Elisa and her parents entered the store, Paul Leff greeted them. "Hello, how may I help you?"

"Our daughter needs glasses, and you have been recommended to us by friends who got their glasses here."

"I'm always happy to hear that! May I see your daughter's prescription? Elisa, I will have to take measurements of your face and eyes."

"This is a waste of time because I won't wear glasses!"

"Why don't you want glasses?" asked Paul. "Wouldn't you like to see better?"

"I don't want to be called a 'four-eyed geek' by my friends!"

"We have frames guaranteed not to make you look like a 'four-eyed geek.' Your appearance is important to you and to us. We have many frames that will look **absolutely fabulous** on you!"

absolutely
definitely, for sure

fabulous
wonderful

"Are there really glasses like that?" Elisa asked hopefully.

"There are many frames in all colors . . . gold, silver, purple . . . . There are all sizes . . . big, small, oval. All kinds.

"May I see the purple ones?" asked Elisa.

"Purple glasses for a very stylish young lady."

"Remember, they have to be *absolutely fabulous* purple!" Elisa smiled for the first time, and her mother breathed a sigh of relief.

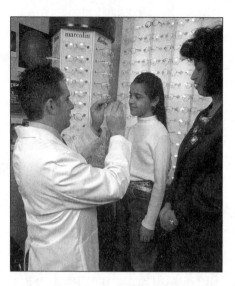

Paul showed Elisa different frames. Some she liked and some she didn't. There wasn't one *absolutely fabulous* pair of frames.

"Elisa, try these on. They're not purple, but I can order them in that color," Paul suggested.

Elisa tried the frames on and thought they looked terrific.

"I like the way these look on me!"

"Elisa, you look like a million dollars and definitely not like a 'four-eyed geek.'"

"Mr. Leff, don't order purple because I like these just the way they are."

relieved *free from worry*

Joan and Miguel were **relieved** that their daughter had found frames she liked. "You look wonderful! Now I know you will wear your glasses."

Elisa Wears Her Glasses

nervous *unsure or uneasy*

Elisa was very **nervous** on her first day at school with her new glasses.

"Sherita, check out how great Elisa's glasses are!" said Amy.

Sherita agreed, "Elisa, you don't look like a *geek* at all."

"I really like the way I look in them. Mr. Leff says these are an *absolutely fabulous* pair of glasses. What do you think, Amy?"

"Absolutely!"

"Sherita?"

"Fabulous!"

Words, Words, Words

A. Read each sentence from the story. Put a √ next to the sentence that gives the correct meaning.

1. Elisa burst through the kitchen door.

   a. _____ Elisa broke her kitchen door.

   b. _____ Elisa rushed through her kitchen door.

2. It's the end of the world!

   a. _____ The situation is so terrible it feels like the world is ending.

   b. _____ The world is coming to an end.

3. We have many frames that will look *absolutely fabulous* on you.

   a. _____ We have many different frames.

   b. _____ We have many frames that will be becoming on you.

4. Elisa, you look like a million dollars.

   a. _____ Elisa was wrapped in a million-dollar bill.

   b. _____ Elisa looked very attractive.

B. A **suffix** is a group of letters added to the end of a word to change its meaning. Read the suffixes and their meanings.

-er means someone who does something
   Joan is a good dancer. (one who dances)

-able means can
   Joan is capable of dancing for hours. (can dance)

-ful means full of
   Elisa is thankful for her friends. (full of thanks)

Word Story:

PIN is short for personal identification number. This pin number can be given for your bank use or in a workplace for security.

-ment means an act or a state of being

Joan signed the agreement with the owner. (an act of agreeing)

Add the correct suffix to the words listed below. Then, write a sentence for each new word.

1. talk _____

_____

2. respect _____

_____

3. truth _____

_____

4. manage _____

_____

C. The letter **y** sometimes has a **long i** vowel sound as in the words *fly* and *cry*. Write the word with the **long i sound** in each sentence. The first one is done for you.

1. He will (try, carry) it later. _____**try**_____

2. Carl didn't know the (lady, spy) in the photo. _____

3. There will be a (study, reply) notice tomorrow. _____

4. The man in the street looked (sly, busy). _____

5. Hillary is going to (bury, buy) the hat. _____

6. Brandon was pointing to the (factory, sky). _____

7. Elisa did not (apply, worry). _____

D. Sometimes the letters **ch** have the sound of **k** as in the word *character*. Put a √ next to the words that have a **k sound.**

1. _____ achieve   2. _____ chorus   3. _____ stomach

4. _____ echo   5. _____ chilly   6. _____ anchor

7. _____ technical   8. _____ chicken   9. _____ choice

Understanding

A. Answer the questions below. Use the story to help you.

1. Elisa and her parents had different feelings about Elisa's need to wear glasses. What were Elisa's feelings?

   _____

   _____

2. What were her parents' feelings?

   _____

   _____

B. Answer the questions below. Use your own ideas.

1. If you had a child who needed glasses, would you behave like Elisa's mother? Yes or No? What would you do the same? What would you do differently?

   _____

   _____

2. What would you do if you needed glasses?

   _____

   _____

3. How do you react to something you do not want to do even though it would be good for you?

   _____

   _____

Discussion

A. Read the questions below. Use the story to find the answers.

1. Why did Joan Vacarro think her daughter needed glasses?

_____

_____

2. What did Mr. Turner notice about Elisa's eyesight?

_____

_____

3. What does *nearsighted* mean?

_____

_____

4. Why did Joan Vacarro choose *Glasses by Paul Leff?*

_____

_____

B. List five things that happened in the story. Then, write a summary paragraph about the story using your list.

1. _____

2. _____

3. _____

4. _____

5. _____

You Can
Solve the Problem

You make choices and solve problems every day. Some choices are automatic and don't require much thought, like stopping a car at a red light or stepping on the gas pedal when the light turns green. Other problems require you to make easy choices, such as which TV show to watch. However, other problems are more difficult to solve. For example, what to say to your teenage son or daughter when he or she comes home past curfew, smelling like beer.

In your life, you will face many problems and choices. You might make good or poor choices because you don't always know how a choice will turn out.

There are some steps you can follow to help you make a good choice and solve your problem. These steps can help you think of options and improve your problem-solving skills. The steps are:

Step 1 Stop and think. Take a deep breath before you say or do something you will regret.

Step 2 Write a problem statement. Be sure to include who has the problem and state it clearly.

Step 3 Write a goal statement. Check to see that it has simple and positive words. For example: I will talk to my son about his grades on Friday evening. I will tell him how proud I am of his efforts. I will ask him how I can help him with his math grade.

Step 4 List all your choices, both the good and the bad choices.

Step 5 Remove choices that don't match your goal, will hurt others, or will cause more problems than they will solve.

Step 6 Make your best choice. Check Step 3 to be sure your choice matches your goal.

A. Read this story.

Linc has been divorced for three years and his children visit every other weekend. When he picked up the children to take them for a weekend recently, his ex-wife told Linc that she was planning to remarry.

Now his children will have a stepfather, and Linc is worried about how everyone will get along. He wants his children to still visit him and enjoy their visits.

B. Can you help Linc solve this problem? Follow the six steps to help Linc make a good choice.

1. What is the first thing Linc should do? (See Step 1)

   _____

2. Write a problem statement.

   _____

   _____

3. What is Linc's goal?

   _____

4. List as many choices as you can for Linc.

   _____

5. Which choices should Linc cross off his list?

   _____

6. What is the best choice for Linc to make?

   _____

7. Does this choice match his goal in Step 3?

   _____

Asking for a Raise

Read how Anthony asks for a raise.

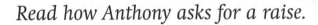

Not a Perfect World

Anthony Fanelli liked to joke that if he ever saw a bird, he probably wouldn't know what he was seeing. That's because Anthony was on his way to work before dawn every day, long before the birds were awake. Most of the time Anthony didn't mind. He liked his job with the **maintenance** department at the Comfort Zone Hotel. The people he worked with were friendly, and his boss, Mr. Kennedy, seemed to like him.

There was a problem, though. Anthony had been employed at the hotel for almost two years, and he had received only one pay raise. Like all new hotel employees, he got that raise after his first six months. He thought he deserved another raise by now and kept waiting for his boss to bring it up. His boss never talked about another raise. He never even hinted at it.

Talking to a Friend

"It just doesn't make sense," Anthony complained one day to his neighbor Nate. "I'm never late for work, and I have called in sick only twice. My supervisor even compliments me sometimes."

maintenance
keeping building, machines, cars in good condition

Nate was working under the hood of his car while he listened to Anthony. He **paused** and looked up at his friend. "Look, man, sounds to me like you have a problem. But I'm not the one you should be telling. You should be telling your boss."

"You mean I should just ask him outright for a raise?" said Anthony.

Nate shrugged. "It sure doesn't sound like you're going to get one any other way. Now hand me that wrench, will you?"

Anthony gave Nate the tool and sighed. "That's not how it's supposed to work. If I do my job well, I shouldn't have to ask for a raise. They should just give me one."

"Yeah, and if I just put gas in my car it should run perfectly all the time, right?"

The two men laughed together. Anthony clapped Nate on the shoulder, then headed home to think.

Easier Said Than Done

One week went by, then another. Anthony had decided to ask for a raise, but it was easier said than done. What if Mr. Kennedy got angry? What if he laughed? Worse, what if he told Anthony to seek employment somewhere else?

paused *stopped for a short time*

One afternoon while Anthony was replacing a light **fixture** in the hotel's dining room, a businessman sat at a table and pulled a pad of paper from his briefcase. The man **rapidly** wrote notes. Then, he took a cellular telephone from his jacket and made a phone call. Anthony wasn't trying to listen in, but it was impossible not to hear what was being said.

"Hi, Curtis!" the man said. "It's me, Raymond. Listen, I think I can close the Benton deal. When I thought about what Mr. Benton said yesterday, I realized that he is really more interested in promise than price. He wanted details about our track record. He also wanted to hear what we could offer his company in the future. So I did two things, Curtis. First, I wrote down notes about our past performance, then I added comments about our planned improvements for next year. I feel better knowing I won't have to walk into our next meeting cold. I'll have facts at my fingertips."

The man chuckled at something Curtis said, then hung up and left. It was nearly 2:30 P.M. Soon, Anthony could clock out and go home to relax. But he wasn't thinking about relaxation. He was thinking about finding some paper and jotting down notes of his own.

Armed With the Facts

By the next morning, Anthony had prepared two pages of notes. He had **rehearsed** so often what he would say to Mr. Kennedy that he felt like an actor learning his lines, but he never got to say them. The minute he asked Mr. Kennedy if they could talk, his boss held up a hand.

"Let me guess," Mr. Kennedy said. "You're either quitting, or you're hitting me up for more money, right?"

Anthony swallowed. "Yes, sir," he said. "It's about the possibility of a raise." He examined his notes. "I'd like to talk about my **contributions** to the hotel and about what I can do in the future."

---

fixture *something that is firmly in place like a door hinge, frying pan handle, or lightbulb socket*

rapidly *quickly*

rehearsed *repeated or practiced something over and over*

contributions *actions, things, or gifts given*

reasonable
*showing good
thinking*

instances
examples

Mr. Kennedy raised an eyebrow. "Hmm . . . that sounds **reasonable,** Anthony. Let's hear what you've got."

For the next 10 minutes, Anthony talked. He pointed out work he had done that went beyond his job description. As an example, he pointed out two **instances** when he was able to repair equipment that Mr. Kennedy had thought would have to be replaced.

"You know, I almost forgot about those," said Mr. Kennedy. "You saved the hotel a heap of money by thinking like that."

"Thank you, sir," said Anthony. He went on to explain ways he thought he could be even more valuable in the future. When he was done, Mr. Kennedy nodded thoughtfully.

"Anthony," he said, "I can't promise you this second that you'll get a raise. First, I have to talk to my own boss. She'll have to check the budget. But you've made some wonderful points, and I think there's reason to be hopeful. You're a good employee, and I want to keep you around for a long time."

The two men shook hands. Anthony put his notes into his pocket and went back to work. He didn't have a raise yet, but he had hope. This was more than he had when he started the day.

Words, Words, Words

A. A **suffix** is a group of letters added to the end of a word. Suffixes change the meaning of the word. For example:

The suffix **-less** means to be without something.
> It was a **windless** day.
>> It was a day without wind.

The suffix **-ful** means full of something.
> He was **hopeful** he would get a raise.
>> He was full of hope that he would get a raise.

Add the suffix **-less** or **-ful** to the underlined words to complete the sentences. The first one is done for you.

1. The sky had no <u>stars</u>. The sky was _____**starless**_____.

2. The movie seemed to have no <u>end</u>. The movie seemed _____.

3. The crime was a <u>shame</u>. The crime was _____.

4. The dress had no <u>straps</u>. The dress was _____.

5. Her <u>glass</u> was filled to the brim with water. She had
   a _____ of water.

6. The man felt no <u>joy</u>. The man was _____.

B. Write the word or words on the line that best complete each sentence. Use the clues in the sentence to help you. The first one is done for you.

1. The mouse ran away when the _____**cat**_____ made a noise.
   > butterfly   wind   cat

2. Anthony's maintenance job included _____.
   > writing letters   changing lightbulbs   planning parties

3. The old woman needed a hearing aid. She could not

_____ what her grandson said without it.

     hear   care   repeat

4. Nate needed a _____ to fix the engine in his car.

     can of paint   seat belt   wrench

5. The salesman often called his steady _____
about his products.

                     repairmen   customers   doctors

C. When the vowel **o** is followed by **w** it often has the same sound as when the **o** is followed by **u.** For example, the words *brown* and *flower* have the same sound as the word *couch.* Read each row of words below. Put a √ next to the two words in each row that have the same vowel sound. The first two are done for you.

1. __√__ couch   _____ touch   __√__ towel

2. __√__ pounce   _____ probe   __√__ prowl

3. _____ elbow   _____ blouse   _____ eyebrow

4. _____ crow   _____ mouse   _____ gown

5. _____ crouch   _____ frown   _____ below

6. _____ ground   _____ growl   _____ group

7. _____ rough   _____ vow   _____ pouch

D. Sometimes two consonants together stand for only one sound. When the letters **sc** are together, sometimes just the **s** sound is heard, as in the word *scissors.* Put a √ next to the words in which only the **s sound** is heard.

1. _____ scarf   2. _____ scope   3. _____ scene

4. _____ escape   5. _____ scent   6. _____ descend

7. _____ science   8. _____ scale   9. _____ muscle

Now write sentences for three of the **s** words.

1. _____

2. _____

3. _____

Understanding

A. Think about the story you just read. Then write answers for the following questions.

1. How were Anthony's mornings different from most people's mornings? _____

_____

2. In what ways were Anthony and the salesman the same?

_____

_____

B. Answer the following questions. Use the story and your own ideas.

1. What are some reasons Anthony might want a raise?

_____

_____

2. What do you think will happen when Mr. Kennedy goes to his own boss about a raise for Anthony?

_____

_____

3. Do you think Mr. Kennedy would one day give Anthony a raise, even if Anthony did not ask for one? Explain your answer.

_____

_____

_____

Discussion

A. Read the sentences below. Write **1, 2, 3,** and **4** to show the order in which things happened in the story.

a. _____ Anthony overheard a businessman on the telephone.

b. _____ Nate listened to Anthony while he worked on his car.

c. _____ Anthony made notes about the work he had done at the hotel.

d. _____ Anthony and Mr. Kennedy talked about a raise.

B. Put a √ next to the **main idea** for each part of the story listed below.

1. The **main idea** for the part called "Not a Perfect World" is

   a. _____ Anthony likes his job.

   b. _____ Nate and Anthony are friends.

   c. _____ Anthony doesn't understand why he hasn't received another raise.

   d. _____ Anthony wants more money.

2. The **main idea** for "Easier Said Than Done" is

   a. _____ Anthony is afraid to ask for a raise.

   b. _____ The businessman wants to get a new customer.

   c. _____ Anthony learns that facts can build confidence.

   d. _____ Anthony's job includes fixing lights.

3. The **main idea** for "Armed With the Facts" is

   a. _____ Mr. Kennedy is a good listener.

   b. _____ Anthony is hopeful about getting a raise.

   c. _____ Mr. Kennedy's boss might not grant Anthony a raise.

   d. _____ Anthony uses facts to make his case for a raise.

You Can
Follow Directions

Bennett bought a deep-blue cotton shirt. He really liked the way it looked on him until he washed it. After he washed it, it did not look good at all. It seemed too small on him, and it was covered with lint. He asked his girlfriend, Shawna, if she thought he should return the shirt.

"How did you wash it?" Shawna asked. "Did you follow the instructions on the label?"

Bennett looked puzzled. "I did not see any instructions on the label here at the collar," he said. "So, I just washed the shirt in hot water with my dark towels. The shirt is dark, too."

Shawna smiled as she showed Bennett the care label in the side seam of the shirt. "Sometimes the instructions are not on the collar's label, Bennett. Read this."

HALTS Men's Wear

SIZE M

Machine wash warm separately
Only non-chlorine bleach
Tumble dry low
Remove promptly
Warm iron if needed
Color may transfer when not
washed before wearing

Use the label to answer the following questions.

1. Do you think Bennett's shirt shrunk because he did not have it dry-cleaned? Yes or No? Explain your answer.

_____

_____

2. At what temperature should Bennett's shirt be washed?

_____

3. Can this shirt be dried in a dryer? Yes or No?

_____

4. What does "Color may transfer when not washed before wearing" mean?

_____

5. What do you think Bennett did that caused his shirt to shrink?

_____

_____

6. If Bennett gets a stain on his shirt, should he use chlorine bleach to remove the stain? Yes or No? Explain your answer.

_____

_____

7. What should Bennett do to prevent his shirt from wrinkling in the dryer?

_____

8. Would you advise Bennett to take his shirt back to the store for a refund? Yes or No? Explain your answer.

_____

9. Where should Bennett look for clothing care labels in the future?

_____

10. What might Bennett do with his new shirt now that it doesn't fit?

_____

At the Tone

Read about using the phone responsibly.

Trouble

"Boy, are you in trouble, little brother." Caitlin Dwyer sat on the front **stoop** and **smirked** at her kid brother, Danny.

Danny stopped bouncing his basketbal. "Is Mom already upstairs? I'm home on time for dinner." Danny **bounded** up the steps bouncing his basketball alongside him. "What do you mean in trouble? And with who?"

"With whom," his sister corrected. "And, you're in trouble with Mom."

"How come? I cleaned my room before I went out to play. I even left a note telling Mom where I was and what time I would be home. So, how come I'm in trouble?"

Caitlin walked ahead of her brother down the hallway to their first-floor apartment. If they listened carefully they could hear the low **murmur** of their neighbors' voices through the apartment doors. They could even smell some of the dinner **aromas** in the hallway, Mrs. Guzman's chili mixed with the heavy scent of Mr. Kelly's Saturday night cabbage.

"So what do you mean I am in trouble with Mom?"

"I think I'll wait for Mom to tell you," she **responded** as she put her key into the door lock. "Hey, Mom, it's me, Caitlin. Danny is here, too." Locking the door behind her, she whispered to her brother, "I don't think you'll be playing basketball for a while."

stoop *small porch and steps in front of an apartment building or house*

smirked *smiled slyly*

bounded *leaped*

murmur *soft noise*

aromas *smells or odors*

responded *answered*

reluctantly *not willing to do something*

Danny's eyes opened wide and turned **reluctantly** to his mother who was standing in the kitchen doorway.

Learning Some Rules

"There you are, young man," Helen Dwyer looked at her son with mixed feelings of **annoyance** and pride. He was growing up to be such a tall, good-looking boy, but he had to learn some **responsibility.**

annoyance *something that bothers you*

responsibility *your duty to do something*

"Told you," Caitlin whispered again as she waved to her mother and started to her room.

"Wait, Caitlin. I think you need to hear this also. Both of you go wash your hands and come into the kitchen."

smugly *with self satisfaction*

Danny looked **smugly** at his sister as she made a face at him. A few minutes later, they sat at the kitchen table and waited to hear what their mother had to say.

Late for Work

"Danny, did your sister tell you that I was late for work today?"

Danny's surprised face turned from his mother to his sister. Late for work! His mother was never late for work. Being on time for work or school was an important rule in their family.

"No, I didn't know. How come you were late?"

"Because of you, stupid!" Caitlin glared at her brother.

"Don't call me. . . ."

"Enough, you two. What did I tell you about calling your brother names? This talk is not about pointing blame. This talk is about following some rules, rules I thought you both understood. Rules that I think we need to go over." Helen Dwyer paused and looked from her son to her daughter. She waited until she knew she had their full attention.

"Sorry, Mom," Caitlin looked sadly at her mother. "It's just that I don't want you to get in trouble with your boss, Mr. Jackson, and lose your job."

"Lose your job!" Danny was confused. What was going on? His sister said he was in trouble. His mother was mad at him, late for work, and now she was going to lose her job.

"Mom, how come you were late for work?"

Telling the Facts

Helen sighed. This wasn't going as she planned. Her husband suggested she wait until he came home from work later tonight, but she wanted to talk with the children sooner. She should just get right to the facts.

"Mr. Jackson wanted me at work an hour earlier today. He had an appointment. I went at my regular time. He almost missed his appointment. He said he had called here this morning and talked to you, Danny. He told you to have me call him if I couldn't get in earlier. When he didn't hear from me, he **assumed** I would be there at the new time."

assumed *believed as true*

Helen looked at her son and waited for him to say something. First, he looked upset, then confused, and then he turned red.

"Oh, gosh, he did call. You and Caitlin were grocery shopping, and Dad was still asleep. I forgot, Mom, I just forgot."

"I know you didn't do this on purpose," Helen patted his arm.

"Are you going to lose your job over this?"

"No, Mr. Jackson was understanding. He's been kind to give me work hours that went along with my class times. But now that I have my GED, I can work full-time. He depends on me. I don't like letting him down."

"I'm really sorry, Mom. Maybe we should get one of those answering machines."

Helen laughed. "I don't think so, Danny. Sometimes we can barely afford the phone bill. No, what I think you and your sister need to remember are the things I told you about when we got the phone back. Do you remember?"

Phone Rules

"Yes, Mom, you said to always answer the phone by saying, 'Hello, the Dwyers. Who is calling?'"

"Exactly," her mother agreed, "and what else?"

Danny piped in, "If they want to speak to you and you can't come to the phone, we should take a message. Uh ohh! I really goofed."

"We all can forget, Danny. So let's see if we can come up with some ways of answering the phone so this won't happen again. After all, you wouldn't want to miss a basketball practice because one of us forgot to give you the message."

So while Helen continued making dinner, they talked. Here are some things they decided to do to become better at using the phone:

1. Place paper and pencil by the phone to write messages.

2. Always get the caller's name and phone number.

3. Repeat the information back to the caller to make sure the name and number are correct.

4. Write down the day and the time that the call came in.

5. If their parents were not at home, they were not to tell this to a stranger.

6. In an emergency, they were to call 911.

When Mr. Dwyer came home from work, Helen and the children told him what they had talked about. Danny again suggested that they get an answering machine. Both his parents said, "Maybe someday." And if they did get one, they promised Danny could record the message.

Words, Words, Words

A. A base of a word is the main part of the word. It is sometimes called the **root word** and a prefix or suffix can be added to it. For example: In the word *quickly,* the base or root word is *quick.* Read the words below. Write the root word on the line. The first one is done for you.

1. lately _____**late**_____   2. bounded _____

3. calling _____   4. looked _____

5. telling _____   6. smugly _____

7. annoyance _____   8. whispered _____

9. playing _____   10. responded _____

Word Story:

Deductions *are the amounts of money taken from your salary. These deductions can be taxes, insurance, or savings.*

B. **Compound words** are two words written together. For example: *Basketball* is a compound word made from the words *basket* and *ball.* Look at the story and find three compound words. Write them on the lines below.

1. I found the following compound words in the story:

   a. _____

   b. _____

   c. _____

Now write the two words that form the compound words on the lines. Then, use each one in a sentence. The first one is done for you.

2. alongside   _____**along**_____   _____**side**_____

   The dog walked alongside the child._____

3. daylight   _____   _____

   _____

4. meatloaf _____   _____

_____   _____

5. makeup _____   _____

_____   _____

C. The **long o** vowel sound is sometimes heard in words with the letters **oa** as in the word *coach*. Read the **long o** words below. Write the word on the line that fits the meaning of each sentence.

soak   soap   throat   cloak   groan   cocoa

1. I washed the dishes with a new _____.

2. Franco wore a black _____ to the party.

3. Peta was not feeling well. She had a sore _____.

4. Jin heard the animal _____ in pain.

5. Katie had to _____ her injured foot every day.

6. My MawMaw likes to drink a hot cup of _____ at night.

D. The letters **ch** sometimes have the sound of **k** as in the word *chorus*. Read the words below. Put a √ next to the words with the **k sound.** Then write a sentence for one of the **k sound** words.

1. _____ chore   2. _____ such   3. _____ chase

4. _____ character   5. _____ chili   6. _____ kitchen

7. _____ machine   8. _____ school   9. _____ children

10. _____

E. You can add **-s** to many words to show more than one. If a word already ends in **-s** or **-ss**, then add **-es.** Write the new word on the line. The first three are done for you.

1. gas _____gases_____   2. grass _____grasses_____

3. lamp _____lamps_____   4. rule _____

5. glass _____   6. aroma _____

7. message _____   8. boss _____

9. illness _____   10. sister _____

Understanding

A. A **fact** is something you know is true from the story. An **opinion** is what you feel or believe. Write **F** for a fact or **O** for an opinion.

1. _____ Answering machines are the best way to answer a phone.

2. _____ Ask callers to repeat their name and number.

3. _____ Caitlin could call 911 in an emergency.

4. _____ Keeping paper and pencil by the phone helps to keep track of phone messages.

5. _____ You should answer the phone with a greeting.

B. Read the sentences below. Put a √ next to the correct answer.

1. Danny came home from

   a. _____ school.   b. _____ playing basketball.

2. Mr. Jackson was

   a. _____ Mrs. Dwyer's boss.   b. _____ Mr. Dwyer's boss.

3. Caitlin was

   a. _____ younger than Danny.   b. _____ older than Danny.

4. The Dwyers lived

   a. _____ on a farm.   b. _____ in an apartment building.

5. Mrs. Dwyer

   a. _____ did finish her GED.   b. _____ did not finish her GED.

Discussion

A. Fill in the circles with ways to use the phone to avoid the problems faced by the Dwyers.

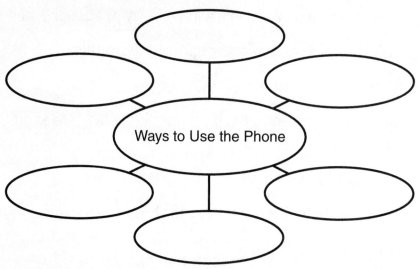

Ways to Use the Phone

B. The word *sequence* means the order in which something happens. Read below about the things that happened in the story. Then, number them in the order they happened.

a. _____ Mr. Dwyer came home from work.

b. _____ Caitlin was sitting on the stoop.

c. _____ Helen Dwyer told Danny why she was late for work.

d. _____ Caitlin unlocked the apartment door.

e. _____ Danny bounded up the stoop with his basketball.

f. _____ Caitlin told her brother he was in trouble.

C. Do you you think the Dwyer family will ever get an answering machine? Explain your answer.

_____

A Closer Look at *Becoming a Voter*

FAMILY LIFE

Now that Neda Kolich is a citizen of the United States and at least 18 years of age, she has the right to vote in the next election. To become a voter, she must also fill out a registration card. After her swearing-in ceremony, she went to the Voter Registration Office. She picked up a voter registration card and filled it out. The card looked like the one on page 58. Use this card to answer the questions. Write your answers on the lines.

1. How many questions must you fill out on this form?

   _____

2. Last name means your family name. Is Kolich a first or a last name? _____

3. What would you fill in for question 2? _____

4. If Neda moved into her new apartment on August 15, 1998, what would she answer for question 8 on the form?

   _____

5. How would Neda answer question 9? (Use the story "Becoming a Citizen of the United States" to help you answer this question.) _____

   _____

6. What would be your answer for question 9? _____

_____

7. Has Neda ever been registered to vote in this county?

_____

8. Why do you think this form asks for a person's height and hair and eye color? _____

9. What is your county of residence? _____

10. How would you answer question 22? _____

PLEASE TYPEWRITE OR HANDPRINT USING BLUE OR BLACK INK.

1. Is This A: ❑ New Registration, ❑ Change of Name, ❑ Change of Address, ❑ Change of Party

2. Print Your Full Name Here _____ **3.** _____
Last Name   First Name (No Nicknames)   Initial   Jr/Sr   Phone No.

4. Full Home Address _____ **5.** _____ **6.** _____
(include APT, and Floor No.)   (City)   ZIP CODE   TOWNSHIP/BORO

4.a If home address is rural route or box number, give nearest cross street, road or highway _____

and nearest public building _____

4.b If you already know your voting district, write it in here _____

7. County of Residence _____ **8.** Date you began address _____
Month/Day/Year

8.a If military, date you left address _____
Month/Day/Year

9. Place of Birth _____ **10.** Date of Birth _____ **11.** Sex _____
(state, territory, or foreign country)   Month/Day/Year

12. Skin Color _____ **13.** Height _____ **14.** Hair Color _____ **15.** Eye Color _____
(optional)

16. In Which Political Party Do You Wish To Be Enrolled? ❑ Democratic ❑ Republican ❑ other _____
(please specify)

17. Have You Ever Registered To Vote Before? Yes ❑ No ❑ If 'yes', complete the following information:

17.a Year of last registration _____ **17.b** Name on last registration _____

17.c County _____

17.d Address on last registration _____ **17.e** State _____ Zip Code _____

18. Do You Require Assistance To Vote? Yes ❑ No ❑ Physical Disability ❑ Illiteracy

❑ Nature of disability _____

PENALTY FOR FALSIFYING DECLARATION
If any person shall sign an official registration application card knowing any statement declared therein to be false, he shall be guilty of perjury, and upon conviction, shall be sentenced to pay a fine not exceeding one thousand dollars ($1,000), or be imprisoned for a term not exceeding five (5) years, or both, at the discretion of the court, in addition, sentence shall include loss of the right of suffrage absolutely for a term of ten (10) years.

NOTARY (USE THIS SPACE ONLY FOR PERSON MAKING MARK)

_____

_____

23. Name and address of person assisting in completion of this form, if applicable.

PLEASE SIGN YOUR NAME THREE TIMES BELOW. THESE SIGNATURES ARE REQUIRED FOR COUNTY REGISTRATION RECORDS. THEN PRINT YOUR NAME ON LINE **22.** IF YOU ARE UNABLE TO SIGN YOUR NAME, SEE INSTRUCTION NO. **3.**

19. X

20. X

21. X _____
(SIGNATURE OF APPLICANT)

22. _____
(PRINTED NAME OF APPLICANT)

LESSON 7

Childhood Immunization

Read how to help children stay free from certain illnesses.

Chester Visits the Clinic

"Well, Mrs. Kyle," said Dr. Ling, "your Chester is as healthy as a horse. He weighs just the right amount for how tall he is. Look how much he's grown since his last checkup! I'd say he's growing like a weed."

"I know," Mrs. Kyle said. "It seems like every other month we have to buy him new clothes." She smiled as she watched Chester playing happily with the blocks on the doctor's examining table.

"There is one thing though, Mrs. Kyle," Dr. Ling said, as he looked at Chester's chart. "Chester has not had all the shots that a four-year-old should have."

"Do you really think that all of those shots are important?" Mrs. Kyle asked.

"Yes, I do," Dr. Ling said. "And, I think that once you realize what each shot does, you will think that they are important, too. I would really like to see that from now on Chester's **immunization** shots are up-to-date."

"Absolutely, Doctor," Mrs. Kyle responded. "I want Chester to stay as healthy as he is now."

immunization
protection against disease or illness through shots

Why Immunize?

Many parents are like Mrs. Kyle in the story. They want their children to be healthy and happy, but they do not realize the importance of the shots given to children. These shots are called immunizations. The purpose of immunizations is to provide the human body with what it needs to fight off illnesses.

Most of the time, immunizations prevent people from ever getting specific diseases. Once in a while, immunized people still get the diseases, but not as badly. Children's health depends on many things. These include

- their diet,
- the amount of exercise they receive,
- how much sleep they get,
- the home **environment,** and, of course,
- the shots they receive.

environment *surroundings*

There are nine **diseases** that can be prevented with **vaccinations.** The first vaccinations are given to children as early as birth. The rest are given as they grow up. Most of the shots are received by the time children are two years of age.

diseases *illnesses or sicknesses*

vaccinations *another word for* immunizations *or shots against certain diseases*

The following information tells about vaccinations and the diseases that they prevent.

The Hepatitis B Vaccination

virus *disease*

The Hepatitis B vaccination (also called HBV) protects children against the Hepatitis B **virus.** This virus affects the liver and can lead to liver cancer. Immunization as an infant can protect a person for his or her entire life.

The DTP Vaccination

The DTP vaccination protects against three diseases. They are diphtheria, tetanus, and pertussis. Diphtheria is a very serious disease. It can make breathing difficult and cause the heart to stop working. About 1 out of every 10 people who get diphtheria die from it.

Tetanus can occur after someone suffers a wound that breaks the skin. If the tetanus germ enters the body at the **site** of the wound, the person may get sick with tetanus. This disease makes swallowing and opening the mouth difficult. Usually, people with tetanus have to stay in the hospital a long time.

Pertussis is sometimes called whooping cough. It causes severe coughing and sometimes choking. This disease makes eating, drinking, and breathing difficult. If not treated soon enough, this disease can cause brain damage.

The Polio Vaccination

The polio vaccination protects against polio. This dangerous disease can make a person unable to walk or move. Also, it can cause breathing problems. There is no cure for polio—only prevention.

The MMR Vaccination

The MMR vaccination also protects against three diseases. They are

1. Measles, which cause a high fever, a cough, and a rash. Sometimes measles can lead to brain damage and hearing loss. Several thousands of cases of measles are treated in the United States each year.

2. Mumps, which cause fever, headache, and **swelling** of the jaw. This disease is easily passed from one person to another. Mumps can lead to hearing loss.

3. Rubella, which is sometimes called German measles. This disease is usually not serious and lasts only a short time. Rubella is most dangerous to pregnant women. Half of the pregnant women who catch rubella will lose their babies or give birth to babies with health problems. Some of the problems these babies suffer include heart disease, blindness, and brain damage. About 1 out of every 10 women in the United States is not protected against rubella.

The HIB Vaccination

The HIB vaccination protects against the HIB disease. This disease is found mostly in children under the age of 5. It often starts out like a cold. Even with quick treatment, 1 out of every 20 children who get HIB will die. Of those who live, many will suffer brain damage.

Side Effects of Vaccinations

The purpose of these shots is to keep children healthy. However, some of these shots have minor side effects. Some children will have a low fever. Some have a loss of energy. Others find that the site of the shot is sore. These problems are common and should not be of concern.

As with any other medical issue, if parents think that anything is wrong after their child gets shots, the doctor should be called. The shots may cause small problems, but their benefits far outweigh their difficulties. Vaccinations are an example of how an ounce of prevention is worth a pound of cure.

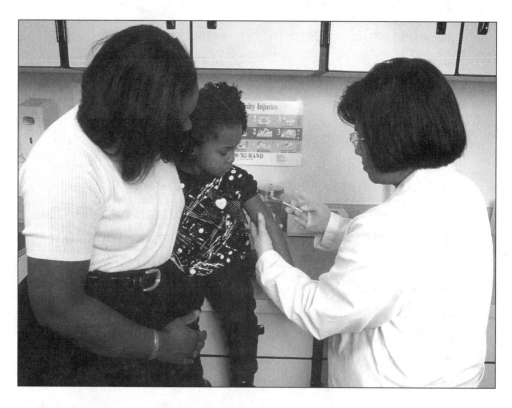

Words, Words, Words

A. Read each sentence below. Put a √ next to the sentence that explains what the line means.

1. "Chester is as healthy as a horse."

   a. _____ Chester is really a horse.

   b. _____ Chester is a very healthy boy.

2. "He's growing like a weed."

   a. _____ He is growing fast.

   b. _____ He is growing so that he looks like a weed.

3. "The jaw may swell as big as a grapefruit."

   a. _____ The jaw will swell to a large size.

   b. _____ You can fit a grapefruit inside your mouth.

B. The words *child's coat* show that the child owns the coat. Add **'s** to a word to show that something is owned. Read the phrases below and add the **'s.**

1. the office in which the doctor works _____

2. the purse that belongs to Mrs. Kyle _____

3. the notebook that was given to Chester _____

4. the arm attached to the doctor _____

5. the shoe that Mrs. Kyle is wearing _____

C. You can add **-s** to most words to show more than one. In the words below, if the word ends in **sh** or **ch** add **-es.** Add **-s** to the other words. Write the new words on the lines.

1. church _____

2. disease _____

3. problem _____

4. brush _____

5. beach _____

6. diet _____

7. shot _____

8. birch _____

D. Two letters in a word can stand for one sound. Put a √ next to the two words in each row that have the same sound.

For example:

_____ bear   __√__ seat   __√__ lean

1. _____ soar   _____ soap   _____ four

2. _____ fruit   _____ loot   _____ loud

3. _____ fool   _____ foal   _____ school

4. _____ rear   _____ wear   _____ deer

E. The consonants **ch** can stand for the sound at the beginning of *chicken* or at the end of *much.* Find some words in the story that have the **ch sound.** Write them on the lines.

1. _____   2. _____

3. _____   4. _____

5. _____   6. _____

7. _____   8. _____

Understanding

A. Answer the questions below.

1. What are the differences between measles and mumps?
   What is the same?

   _____

   _____

2. What one thing is the same for both pertussis and diphtheria?
   What is different?

   _____

   _____

B. Read the sentences below. Put a √ next to the best endings for them.

1. The purpose of immunizations is to

   a. _____ cure someone who is sick.

   b. _____ keep someone from getting sick.

   c. _____ make people happy.

2. The health of a child depends on many things. One of those things is

   a. _____ the color of his or her eyes.   b. _____ his or her age.

   c. _____ his or her diet.

3. Hepatitis B affects the liver. It can then lead to

   a. _____ liver cancer.   b. _____ loss of eyesight.

   c. _____ broken bones.

Discussion

A. Read the questions below. Use the story to help you find answers.

1. Against what three diseases does the DTP vaccination protect?

_____

_____

_____

2. What is another name for rubella? _____

3. Polio can cause two different problems for a person. What are they? _____

4. List three minor problems a child may have as a result of vaccinations. _____

_____

_____

B. When you talk about **cause** and **effect,** you are talking about something that happens and then what happens because of it. Read the example below. Then, find two more examples of cause and effect from the story and list them.

	Cause	Effect
1.	Chester grew since his last checkup.	The doctor commented about his size.
2.	_____	_____
	_____	_____
3.	_____	_____
	_____	_____

LESSON 8

Grandma's Dying Wish

Read about the importance of a mammogram.

Courage

This is a story about a woman with **inoperable cancer** of the breast. It is not a story about her courage, though she has plenty. It is not a story about her will to live, though she fights for her life each day. Rather, it is a story about her dying wish. She wants her only granddaughter, Vivian, to know how to prevent inoperable breast cancer. She really wants Vivian to know the importance of a **mammogram.**

As many grandmas know, when a girl is only 19, she does not think of her own death. She is just becoming an adult. At this age, people tend to think "nothing bad can happen to me." They think they are too young and too strong. Also, as grandmas know, when you talk to a 19-year-old about death, the next day most of what you said is forgotten. For the next day holds more pressing issues—a final exam or a Saturday night date.

Vivian's grandma didn't want her to forget what she had to say, so she didn't pick up the phone. Instead, she took a pen in her slightly **trembling** hand and wrote the most important letter she'd ever written.

inoperable cancer *cancer which has reached such a serious state that it cannot be removed through an operation*

mammogram *a medical test in which the breast is viewed by X ray*

trembling *shaking*

My Dearest Vivian,

I know that what I am about to tell you, you may not want to hear. But I beg that you read this letter from start to finish. If you do nothing about it today, put it in your jewelry box. Then, each year on my birthday, read it. It is my prayer that one day the contents of this letter will no longer be written only on these sheets but will be written on your heart. For then, you will do as I should have done years ago.

As you know, I am dying of breast cancer. I should have found out about it earlier. Then it may have been treatable.

As a young woman, there are many things you can do to lead a healthy life. Diet and exercise are important. But as you grow older, diet and exercise will not be enough. You must do what you can to be aware of what is going on within your body. Regular checkups should remain part of your life. And as you get older, regular mammograms will become vital to your health.

Let me tell you abot a mammogram. This is a text used to see if you have breast cancer. Very simply, it is an X ray of the breast. This test can find breast **cancer masses** that are too small for you or your doctor to feel. In fact, it can find cancer up to two years before you can feel a lump. My

cancer masses
clumps of cancer cells

dear, when breast cancer is found this early, chances for survival are the greatest.

The test is so simple. There is no reason not to do it. During the test, you will stand in front of an X-ray machine. The person who runs the test will place your breast between two plastic plates. Then he or she will squeeze the plates toward each other. This flattens the breast between them. With the breast tissue flattened, an X ray is taken. I know, this sounds uncomfortable. It will only be so for a few seconds. But it is needed to get a good picture. Two pictures will be taken of each breast. One picture will be taken from the top. The other will be taken from the side. The entire test takes about 15 minutes. Just think, a 15-minute test could add years to your life.

I am not trying to scare you, but there is more you should know. Of all cancers, this one is the leader for killing women. Women most at risk will have a mother, a sister, or a daughter with cancer.

The chance of getting breast cancer increases with age. That is why the American Cancer Society recommends that every woman have a mammogram at age 40. The test should be repeated every year or two until age 49. After age 50, the test should be done each year.

Women of all ages should have a physical breast exam once a year. During this test, a doctor will feel the breast tissue by hand. If any lumps are felt, a mammogram may be ordered.

I know that what I am about to tell you may sound like a waste of time. But, my dear child, it is not. I want you to make a point of doing a self-exam each month. Use your hand to feel the tissue of each breast for any lumps, thickness, or other changes. If you find anything unusual, call your doctor at once.

It is too late for me to change my future. But, you have yours ahead of you. Take care of it.

Love,

Grandma

Breast Cancer Facts

Breast cancer is an important health issue. However, it is not just a woman's health issue. Men can also become victims of breast cancer. It does not happen frequently, but it can happen. Men over 50 and men with a family history of breast cancer should be alert to the same signs of breast cancer as women.

One in eight women will develop breast cancer during her lifetime. Taking the time for a mammogram may save your life. This simple test can show cancer up to two years before a lump can be felt. Remember, breast cancer is not a woman's health issue, it is a family issue.

Some early signs to look for are:

1. a lump or thickening in the breast or under the arm, or

2. a change in the shape of the breast, or

3. discharge from the nipple, or

4. a change in the color or feel of the breast or the nipple area.

Words, Words, Words

A. Read the sentences below. Write the word or words that each underlined word stands for. The first one is done for you.

1. Grandma knew <u>she</u> was dying. _____**she stands for Grandma**_____

2. Vivian received a letter from her grandma. <u>It</u> was an important letter. _____

3. Vivian put the letter in her jewelry box. Each year on her grandma's birthday, she read <u>it</u>. _____

4. The jewelry box was very old. <u>It</u> was a gift. _____

5. Mammograms are medical tests. <u>They</u> are x rays of the breast.

_____

Word Story:

Net pay *is the paycheck amount you take home after all deductions are made.*

B. Read each sentence. Look for the underlined word. Put a √ next to the word or words that mean the same. The first one is done for you.

1. The scarf was a bright <u>orange.</u>

   a. _____ a fruit to eat

   b. __√__ a color

2. Turn <u>left</u> at the stop sign.

   a. _____ something remaining

   b. _____ a direction to travel

3. The cowboy roped a <u>steer.</u>

   a. _____ a cow

   b. _____ to guide a car

4. We threw pennies in the wishing well.

    a. _____ to be healthy

    b. _____ a place to get water

C. The vowels **ou** can stand for the sound in *cloud* or the sound in *cousin*. Put a √ next to the words in the row that have the same vowel sound.

    Example:

__√__ enough	_____ young	__√__ tough
1. _____ pound	_____ sound	_____ rough
2. _____ couple	_____ proud	_____ trouble
3. _____ double	_____ house	_____ loud
4. _____ spouse	_____ plough	_____ touch
5. _____ couch	_____ pouch	_____ court

D. The consonant **c** can have the sound of **s** as in *ice* or of **k** as in *cat*. Say the words below. Write **s** or **k** on the line to show the sound of **c**. Hint: Sometimes a word can have both sounds.

1. _____ courage	2. _____ importance
3. _____ becoming	4. _____ cage
5. _____ contents	6. _____ exercise
7. _____ cash	8. _____ cancer
9. _____ concern	10. _____ caring

E. Add **-s** or **-es** to each word to make it mean more than one. If the word ends in **s,** or **ss,** add **-es.** Add **-s** to the other words. Write the new words on the lines.

1. gas _____

2. partner _____

3. class _____

4. letter _____

5. adult _____

Understanding

A. A **fact** is something you know is true. An **opinion** is what you feel or believe. Write **F** if the sentence is a fact. Write **O** if the sentence is an opinion.

1. _____ One in nine women will get breast cancer.

2. _____ Mammograms take about 15 minutes to complete.

3. _____ It hurts when you get a mammogram.

4. _____ The chances of getting breast cancer increase with age.

5. _____ Teenagers are not mature enough to think about death.

6. _____ Women of all ages should have a physical breast exam once a year.

7. _____ A mammogram can find breast cancer masses that are too small for you or your doctor to feel.

8. _____ Breast cancer is a leading killer of women.

9. _____ Women most at risk for getting breast cancer have a female relative—grandmother, mother, sister—with cancer.

10. _____ Since you see a doctor once a year, you don't need to do a monthly breast self-exam.

B. What are some of the early warnings of breast cancer?

_____

_____

_____

_____

Discussion

A. Decide what the **main idea** is for each part of the story below. Put a √ next to your answer.

1. The **main idea** of "Courage" is

   a. _____ Grandma wishes that she was not dying.

   b. _____ Grandma wishes that her granddaughter was not dying.

   c. _____ Grandma wishes that her granddaughter would know how to prevent inoperable breast cancer.

2. The **main idea** of "The Letter" is

   a. _____ Grandma knows that what she is saying is unpleasant.

   b. _____ Grandma is begging Vivian to take care of herself.

   c. _____ Grandma wants to tell her granddaughter what having cancer is like.

3. The **main idea** of "About Mammograms" is

   a. _____ mammograms are difficult to have.

   b. _____ mammograms are vital in detecting breast cancer.

   c. _____ mammograms are painful.

B. A **cause** is what makes something happen. An **effect** is what happens. Read the sentences below. Write **C** next to the cause. Write **E** next to the effect.

1. _____ Grandma did not get a routine mammogram.

   _____ She found out too late that she had breast cancer.

2. _____ She doesn't think about her own death.

   _____ The granddaughter in this story is only 19.

A Closer Look at Food Labels

Catherine knows that fresh fruits and vegetables are good for her health. She likes fresh fruits and vegetables and tries to eat them every day. But, one day she finds oranges in a can. They are called Mandarin oranges.

Catherine thinks they look tasty and might be good tossed in a lettuce salad. However, she wonders if they are nutritious. She looks at the label where she sees **Nutrition Facts.** She reads these facts carefully before she buys the Mandarin oranges. The label she read appears on this page.

Varca

QUALITY GUARANTEED
WHOLE PEELED
Mandarin Orange
SEGMENTS IN LIGHT SYRUP

Nutrition Facts
Serving Size ⅔ cup (150g)
Servings Per Container about 2

Amount Per Serving

Calories 90   Calories From Fat 0

% Daily Values*

Total Fat 0g	0%
Saturated Fat 0g	0%
Cholesterol 0mg	0%
Sodium 20mg	1%
Total Carbohydrate 20g	7%
Dietary Fiber 0g	0%
Sugars 20g	
Protein 1g	

Vitamin A 6% • Vitamin C   35%
Calcium 2% • Iron 4%

* Percent Daily Values are based on a 2,000 calorie diet.

INGREDIENTS: PEELED MANDARIN ORANGE SEGMENTS, WATER, SUGAR.

DISTRIBUTED BY THE VARCA CO.,
BUFFALO, NY
PRODUCT OF CHINA

USES: Mandarin Orange Segments are delicious for appetizer, salad or dessert. Excellent in combination with such fruits as apricots, bananas or grapefruit sections, or with cheese, or to surround gelatin molds. Use them in gelatin desserts, in fruit cocktail and fruit salads.

Use the label to help you answer the following questions.

1. What vitamins are found in this can of Mandarin oranges? _____

_____

2. How much cholesterol is in this fruit? _____

3. Has sugar been added to this can of fruit? How do you know?

_____

4. What else has been added to the oranges? _____

5. Is this canned fruit a good source of protein? Yes or No? Explain your answer. _____

_____

6. Would you recommend this fruit to someone on a fat-free diet? Why or why not? _____

_____

7. Catherine decided the Mandarin oranges were nutritious. Do you agree with her? Yes or No? Explain your answer. _____

_____

_____

8. Do you think it would be better if Catherine used a fresh orange in her salad? Explain your answer. _____

_____

_____

9. Catherine wants to mix the oranges with lettuce to make a salad. What else could Catherine make with these oranges?

_____

_____

10. Where are these Mandarin oranges grown? Hint: Look carefully at the label. _____

A Healthy Birthday Party

NUTRITION · HEALTH AND SAFETY

Would you like to give a healthy birthday party for a child? Read how Mara gave one for her daughter, Tashi.

Meet Mara

Mara and her husband are from **Pakistan.** Their daughter, Tashi, goes to a day care center while Mara attends an adult education program and her husband works. At the program, Mara is learning English and work skills. Mara is also learning about **nutrition.** She is learning that adults and children should eat good food to stay healthy. These foods help young and old bodies grow strong and fight disease.

What Mara Learned

In the nutrition class, Mara learned that vegetables, fruits, and grains are important to a healthy eating plan. A good eating plan is a good diet. Mara became so interested in good eating that she decided she wanted to study English as much as she could. She wanted to become a **nutritionist** in a hospital or a nursing home. She would have to wait to work in this field until Tashi was a little older, but she could still take all the classes now to learn about nutrition.

Pakistan *an independent country in South Asia on the Arabian Sea. The capital is Islamabad. Pakistan is about the size of the state of Texas.*

nutrition *healthy foods*

nutritionist *a person who studies about nutrition and helps other people to learn to eat healthy foods*

77

Tashi's Birthday

When it was time for Tashi's fourth birthday, Mara decided to practice what she had learned about good food. She decided to make food for Tashi and the other children in the day care center that they would enjoy eating and that would also be good for them.

protein *necessary parts in food for the body's growth*

Mara decided to serve some vegetables, fruits, grains, and also some **protein** to help build their muscles. Mara cut up some nice fresh green peppers into pieces the children could eat with their fingers. This was one of the vegetables, along with celery and carrots, that she brought to Tashi's birthday party.

Mara also selected fruits. She chose apples, oranges, pineapples, and bananas. Pineapples and bananas are fruits that people in her home in Pakistan liked to eat. Mara chose apples and oranges because they are popular fruits with American children. She cut the fruit into pieces the children could easily eat.

prepared *made ready*

Although Tashi was going to be four years old, this was the first party she was having at the day care center. Mara wanted it to be special so she **prepared** a special dish from Pakistan. It was a **pudding** made with brown rice, raisins, nuts, and milk.

pudding *sweet dessert*

Mara knew that brown rice and nuts are grains and would provide protein in the children's diet. Mara also put honey into the pudding to make it sweet so the children would like the taste.

spices *flavorings*

To add more protein to the party diet, Mara made a small piece of chicken for each child to eat. She baked the chicken in special Pakistan **spices.** She was careful how much she used because she didn't want the spices to be too strong for the children. She wanted the children to enjoy the chicken.

The Birthday Cake

Mara asked herself, "How could there be a birthday party without a birthday cake?" She had learned about angel food cake in her nutrition class. Angel food cake is made with many whites of eggs but with no egg yolks. Egg yolks have many good things in them, but they also have a lot of fat. Mara did not want to give the children too much fat. The egg whites in the angel food cake would give them a lot of protein without giving them too much fat.

Mara also made a special frosting. She used powdered sugar and low-fat butter. She flavored the icing with a little lemon peel so that it would taste good.

Lunch Time

Mara had talked with the day care staff about the party. They knew she would be bringing all the food for lunch on the day of Tashi's birthday.

When the special day arrived, Mara brought all the food to the center at noon. The children were ready to have a party for Tashi. That morning, Mara dressed Tashi in a **sari** that she had made. This sari dress was what girls in Pakistan wear.

Tashi was very happy with her bright sari dress. Mara also wore a sari dress in the same color as Tashi's. The day care teacher, Mrs. Owens, made a crown for Tashi.

sari *the main clothing worn by women in Pakistan. It is a long piece of cotton, silk, or other fabric.*

The most important part of the party was the good food. The children liked the vegetables. They ate the green peppers, carrots, and celery pieces. They enjoyed the vegetables and all the pretty colors.

The children also ate the fruits. The apples, oranges, pineapple, and banana pieces would help to keep them healthy because they contained vitamins. They also contained crunchy **fibers.**

fibers *roughage that helps you digest your food*

The special treat was the pudding. Mrs. Owens told them that the pudding had brown rice in it. Mara told them that brown rice pudding is an important part of the Pakistan diet. The children also learned that brown rice and nuts have proteins.

Mara served the brown rice and nut pudding in paper cups. The children ate their pudding with spoons. They also ate the chicken. Everyone enjoyed the pieces of chicken and asked for more. Mara had made plenty of food and was happy to see the children enjoy it.

When it came time for the cake, the children were surprised to see an angel food cake. But the angel food cake was sweet, and the icing was **delicious.** Mara put four candles on the cake for Tashi to blow out. Tashi made a wish and blew out all the candles. All the children clapped their hands.

delicious *tastes very good*

Birthday Wish

Later that night, Tashi told her mother and father what she had wished for. She wished her mother would learn all about good foods to eat so that she could help more people grow strong and healthy.

Mara said that was why she was working hard to read and write English. She wanted to read more books about nutrition and good food.

Words, Words, Words

A. Put a √ next to the **synonym** for the underlined word.

1. Mara learns <u>work</u> skills.
   a. _____ diet   b. _____ job   c. _____ health

2. Mara and Tashi each wore a <u>sari</u> for the party.
   a. _____ hat   b. _____ apron   c. _____ dress

3. Mara baked the chicken with <u>spices</u>.
   a. _____ flavorings b. _____ vegetables c. _____ apples

B. Put a √ next to the **antonym** for the underlined word.

1. The children could <u>easily</u> eat the pieces of fruits.
   a. _____ cut up   b. _____ at rest   c. _____ with difficulty

2. Mara made the angel food cake <u>sweet</u>.
   a. _____ strong   b. _____ sour   c. _____ healthy

3. Mara <u>remembered</u> lunch was at noon at the day care.
   a. _____ cooked   b. _____ left home c. _____ forgot

C. The letters **wr** together can make the sound of **r** as in the word *wrong*. Circle the word that best fits the meaning for each sentence.

1. The skirt was (wrinkled, wrinkles) when I took it from the suitcase.

2. My neighbor broke her (wrist, wreck) in a car (wrist, wreck).

3. He belongs to the first level (wrestled, wrestling) team.

4. I will attach the red bow to the (wreath, wrath).

D. Draw a line from a word in Column 1 to a word in Column 2 to make a compound word. Use each new compound word in a sentence.

Column 1	Column 2
wind	quake
book	shake
human	shield
neck	shelf
earth	lace
milk	kind

1. _____

2. _____

3. _____

4. _____

5. _____

6. _____

E. The suffix **-ed** added to a word can sometimes make the word tell about something that has happened. Add the suffix **-ed** to the following words. Write a sentence for each word.

For example: She play**ed** the game yesterday.

1. work _____   _____

2. enjoy _____   _____

3. chew _____   _____

4. learn _____   _____

5. want _____   _____

F. You can add **-s** to many words to say more than one. If a word ends with the letter **x**, add **-es** to say more than one. Write the new words on the lines.

1. fox _____   2. finger _____

3. fiber _____   4. tax _____

5. vitamin _____   6. six _____

McGraw-Hill/Contemporary Essentials of Reading   Book 6

Understanding

A. Read the sentences below. Tell in your own words why Mara did what she did. You can also use the story to help you. The first one is done for you.

1. Mara wanted to study about healthy food so _____

   she could be a nutritionist and work in a hospital or nursing home.

2. Mara wanted to bring healthy food to her daughter's birthday party because _____

   _____

3. For some of the fruits she brought for the party, Mara chose bananas and pineapples because _____

   _____

4. Mara cut the vegetables into small pieces because _____

   _____

5. Mara and Tashi wore saris to the party because _____

   _____

B. Use the story and your own ideas to answer the questions below.

1. Do you think the angel food cake was a good choice for a birthday cake? Yes or No? Explain your answer. _____

   _____

2. What are some things or new ideas the children might have learned from Tashi's party? _____

   _____

Discussion

A. A **cause** makes something happen. An **effect** is the result from the cause. Read the sentences below. Write the cause on the **Cause** line. Write the effect on the **Effect** line.

1. Mara flavored the icing with lemon peel so it would taste good.

    Cause: _____

    Effect: _____

2. She cut the celery into bright, pretty pieces for the children to eat with their fingers.

    Cause: _____

    Effect: _____

3. Mara put honey in the pudding to make it sweet.

    Cause: _____

    Effect: _____

B. Use the story to answer the questions below.

1. What was Mara's main reason for studying to become a nutritionist in a hospital or nursing home?

    _____

    _____

2. What was the main reason Tashi wished that her mother would be able to learn to work as a person who plans healthy food?

    _____

    _____

You Can
Tell What's Happening

Pictures can tell stories without using any words. The picture below tells its own story. Study the picture. Then, continue to read.

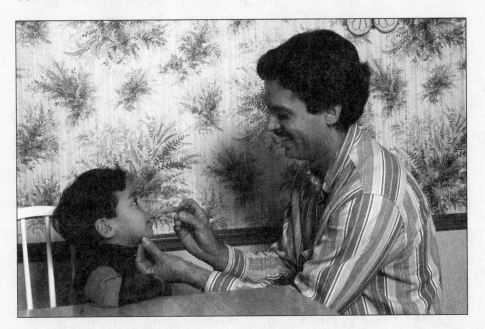

A. Did you think the picture is telling a story about a young father giving his son some medicine?

At first glance, it probably does look like that. However, if you thought more about it, you might think about the events that led up to giving the child his medicine. You could ask yourself such questions as:

- Was the little boy very ill?
- Did they take the little boy to the doctor?
- What did the father do to make sure the medicine was correct?

There is a lot that is going on in the picture.

What should you do when you have to give or take medicine? How do you make sure the medicine is correct? Here are some things to think about.

1. Ask the doctor or pharmacist about the medicine and how it should be taken.
2. Tell the doctor what other medicines you or your child is taking.
3. Get childproof caps on your medicines.
4. Read carefully the directions on all medicines.
5. Do not read labels or try to administer the medicines in the dark.
6. Never call medicine "candy."
7. Use the original holders for medicines. Never put pills into other household containers.

B. Now answer some questions about the picture.

1. Where do you think the picture was taken? _____

2. How many people are in the picture? _____

3. What are they doing? _____

C. Now, write a story about what is happening in the picture. There are lots of things to write about. Give the people names. Tell what may have happened before the picture was taken. Tell what may have happened after the picture was taken.

_____

_____

_____

_____

Being a Nutritionist

Read about a job that helps people learn to eat well and stay healthy.

Changes in the Way We Eat

Our busy lives have changed the way we eat and think about food. In past times, families ate most of their meals together. It was usual for every family member to be home at dinner. Dinner was the biggest meal of the day. It gave people most of their day's nutrition.

In today's society, people don't always have time for a big dinner. They often eat at fast-food restaurants.

Fast foods are foods that can be eaten quickly. They are often eaten with the hands. Foods like hamburgers, hot dogs, nachos, and french fries are fast foods. Fast foods are often higher in fat and lower in nutrition than foods made at home.

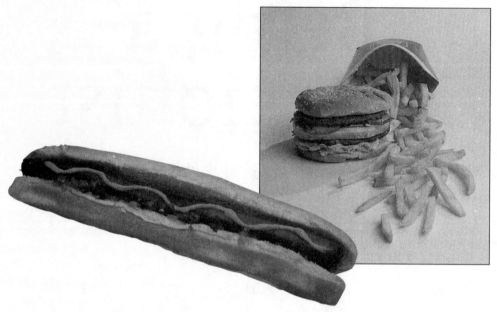

Today's families also buy other foods that are cooked at the store and then taken home. Precooked foods may lose nutrition when they are heated a second time. Since many families today eat this way, they may not be getting all the nutrition they need to stay healthy.

People Who Can Help

There are people who help other people learn how to choose healthy foods to eat. These people are called nutritionists. There are several kinds of jobs that nutritionists do.

dietician *a nutritionist who has had four years of college and can work with special food needs for people in hospitals and nursing homes*

The job of **dietician** is the hardest type of job to get. Dieticians are nutritionists who work in hospitals, schools, or nursing homes. They help people with illnesses who need to eat special kinds of foods. Dieticians have special training about nutrition and healthy eating. Dieticians go to college for four years. Then, they work with other dieticians for one year to learn the job. After all this, they must pass a state test before they can be called a dietician.

Dieticians talk to **patients** to see what they like to eat and to tell them about healthy eating. To help a patient, dieticians make up special food lists. Sometimes the patient cannot eat sugar or salt. The patient may need to eat only soft foods or foods cooked a special way.

patients *people who are receiving care in a hospital or a nursing home*

Other Helpers

Some people are helpers to dieticians. These are **dietary technicians**. Dietary technicians often work in hospitals and nursing homes, too. Both dieticians and dietary technicians help patients get the right foods to eat. The dietary technician tells the cafeteria what the dietician wants. The dietary technician sees to it that the foods are cooked right. The dietary technician may check to see that the patient eats the special foods and not other foods. The dietary technician may see that a patient does not eat as much of a certain food. The patient may be eating more of another food. Then the dietary technician can tell the dietician that changes may need to be made on the food list.

dietary technicians *people who do a special job, usually helping a nutritionist*

To be a dietary technician, you must attend college for two years, not four years. Dietary technicians take classes to teach them about nutrition. They must learn about healthy eating. When they are done, they can go right to work. They do not have to take or pass a state test.

Food Service Workers

There are other jobs for people who like to help people be healthy. These jobs are also for people who like to work with food. The job of food service worker is one such job. Food service workers

- serve foods to people,
- place food on plates or trays,
- help make some foods,
- keep foods hot or cold as needed,
- keep the serving area clean and safe for serving food.

When doing their tasks, they must be careful to have clean hands at all times. They must wear hair nets to keep their hair from falling into the foods they serve. Food service workers help keep people healthy by safely serving nutritious foods.

You do not need a college degree to be a food service worker. You can become a food service worker with a high school diploma or a GED. Food service jobs are available in cafeterias, schools, nursing homes, or hospitals.

Nutrition Educators

Some nutritionists work as teachers. They teach people about eating well and practicing good nutrition habits. Some nutrition teachers work at weight-loss **clinics.** They help people learn to eat healthy foods so they can lose weight.

clinics *places where people go to receive special care other than a hospital or a nursing home*

Some nutritionist educators work one-on-one with people. They help people see how to improve their nutrition and to avoid the mistakes they may be making with their nutrition. Nutrition educators help people make decisions about healthy eating changes and how to carry them out.

Nutrition educators usually take special classes. Even though there are no special conditions for nutrition educators, they often go to college. If you are interested in this field, you can check with your own state about its laws. You can find out if there are any state rules about becoming a nutrition educator.

If you like to work with food and to help people stay healthy, there are many jobs you can do. This story tells about only a few. One of these jobs or some other job in the field of food service may be the right one for you.

Words, Words, Words

A. Read the sentences below. Look for the underlined word. Write the word or words from the sentences that explain the underlined word. The first one is done for you.

1. Dinner was the biggest meal of the day. <u>It</u> provided the largest source of the day's nutrition. _____**dinner**_____

2. Sometimes parents are too tired to cook. <u>They</u> may bring home food from a fast-food restaurant. _____

3. The cafeteria served hot dogs, hamburgers, nachos, and french fries tonight. <u>These</u> are the kinds of foods that fast food restaurants sell. _____

4. People may not eat the kinds of foods <u>they</u> need to stay healthy. _____

5. Nutritionists can be dieticians, dietary technicians, or food service workers. <u>Some</u> may also be educators. _____

B. Add **'s** to show that something belongs to one person. Add **s'** to show that something belongs to more than one person. For example:

> The words *aunt's car* mean the car belongs to one aunt.
> The words *aunts' car* mean the car belongs to more than one aunt.

Add **'s** or **s'** to the words below to show ownership. Write your answers on the lines.

1. the food belongs to a restaurant

_____

2. the job belongs to a food service worker

_____

3. the meals belong to many families

_____

4. the helpers belong to several hospitals

_____

5. the trays belong to the cafeteria

_____

C. The letter **y** can have a **long i sound** as in the word *cry*. Sometimes it has a **long e sound** as in the word *lady*. Read the list of words below. Write the **long i** words under the word *cry*. Write the **long e** words under the word *lady*.

try   healthy   hurry   my   dietary   buy   every   why

cry	**lady**
_____	_____
_____	_____
_____	_____
_____	_____
_____	_____

D. Sometimes two letters can stand for one sound. The letters **mb** sometimes have the sound of **m,** as in the word *comb*. Put a √ next to the words in which the **mb** has the **m sound.**

1. _____ tomb   2. _____ crumble   3. _____ member

4. _____ plumber   5. _____ timber   6. _____ limber

7. _____ slumber   8. _____ rumble   9. _____ dumb

10. _____ emblem   11. _____ comb   12. _____ bamboo

13. _____ gamble   14. _____ ramble   15. _____ lamb

16. _____ jamboree   17. _____ combination   18. _____ thumb

McGraw-Hill/Contemporary Essentials of Reading   Book 6

Understanding

A. Answer the following questions.

1. Give two reasons why many of today's families do not eat large dinners together as the families did in the past.

   _____

   _____

2. Give two reasons why many people today may not get proper nutrition from the foods they eat. _____

   _____

   _____

3. What might happen if a food service worker wanted to become a dietary technician? Name two things he or she might need to do. _____

   _____

   _____

B. Do you think most families would like to have more old-time family dinners together? Yes or No? Explain your answer.

   _____

   _____

   _____

   _____

   _____

Discussion

A. Read each question below. Use the story to help you give answers.

1. Some people can eat a lot of food but still not be healthy. What are they missing in the foods they eat? _____

    _____

2. What do you call people who help other people to choose healthy foods to eat and stay well? _____

    _____

3. Name three jobs that people who like to help others eat healthy foods might do. _____

    _____

    _____

    _____

B. Put a √ next to your answers. Use the story to help you.

1. What is the main idea of "Changes in the Way We Eat"?

    a. _____ There are changes in the way people eat today, such as eating more *fast food.*

    b. _____ There are changes in the way people eat today, such as eating more foods from their gardens.

2. What is the main idea of the part called "People Who Can Help"?

    a. _____ It is about people who help other people make food.

    b. _____ There are many different jobs for people called nutritionists.

LESSON 11

Savita Gets a Job in Food Service

Read about Savita and her new job as a food service worker. Find out what skills are needed to work as a food service worker.

Getting an Interview

Today is Savita's lucky day. When she looked at the want ads this morning, she saw an ad for a job she thought would be right for her. The ad was for a food service worker in a nursing home.

Savita dialed the number and spoke to a woman in the personnel office. She told the woman she was interested in the opening for a food service worker. The woman told Savita that the worker must be 18 years of age or older and had to have a high school diploma or a GED.

"I am over 18," said Savita, "and I received my GED last summer."

"Then please come in and fill out an **application** tomorrow morning at 10," said the woman on the phone. "Do you need directions on how to get here?"

application a form that contains information about you that you fill out in order to be interviewed for a job

"Yes," answered Savita, and she listened carefully and wrote down the directions.

After she hung up, Savita breathed a long sigh. "Well, that step is taken," she thought. "Now I'm ready for the next step."

Getting Ready for the Interview

The next morning, Savita dressed carefully for the interview. She put on a **conservative** but nice-looking dress. She arranged her hair and makeup so she looked neat and clean. She knew that neatness and **cleanliness** were important when working around food. She wanted the **interviewer** to think of her as a good choice for this job.

At the Interview

Savita arrived at the nursing home on time for her interview. She met Judi Rockwell, the woman she had spoken to on the phone.

"Thank you for coming so **promptly**," Judi said to Savita as she showed her into a small office. "Please have a seat, and let's talk about why you think you'd like to be a food service worker."

"Well, first of all," said Savita, "I love to cook and serve food. I love to make plates look pretty. I thought this job would let me do some of those things."

"I see," said Ms. Rockwell. "That's a great attitude, but how do you feel about working with older people?"

"I love older people," said Savita. "I loved it when my grandmother lived with us. I used to cook her favorite dishes and serve them to her. Sometimes I helped her cut up her food, too."

"It sounds like you are a caring person, Savita," said Ms. Rockwell. "That is an important attitude when someone works with older people. Now, what hours can you work? And would you have a ride to work?"

conservative *traditional, businesslike, not flashy or fancy*

cleanliness *being clean, not dirty*

interviewer *a person who asks questions of someone trying to get a job*

promptly *in a short time; on time*

A Job Offer

Savita answered several other questions before the interview was over.

"I think you would be a great person for this job, Savita," Ms. Rockwell said. "You can start next Monday, but first you'll need to fill out these papers. You will also need some uniforms, and you will need to get a physical **exam.** This is done for all people who work with food."

exam *a test*

Job Training

Bright and early the following Monday, Savita started her new job. She met Jimmy Daley, who was the **supervisor** in charge of training new workers. Jimmy showed Savita how to set the cooked foods on the service line. Some food went over pans of very hot water. Some went over pans of ice. He showed Savita how much food to place on the plates. Jimmy showed her how to use gloves so that her hands would not touch the food people would eat.

job training *teaching that shows how to do a certain job*

supervisor *the person in charge; the boss*

Finally, someone came through the food line. "Good afternoon," Savita said as she dished out the food. "I hope you're having a nice day today."

"Why yes, I am," said the elderly man. He smiled at Savita.

Job Changes

Within a few months, Savita had learned the names of the people who came through her line. She greeted each with a smile. Savita felt she had found her place. She loved working in the nursing home, but she felt that she wanted to do more. Savita asked her supervisor, Jimmy, if she could start serving some meals to the patients in their rooms. She could help patients set up their beds and fix the trays on the bed tables.

Savita also started to learn more about nutrition. She talked to the dietician about nutrition and healthy eating. Savita thought she might want to become a dietary technician. She knew she would have to go to college. It would be hard, but she really wanted to move up in the work she had chosen.

Savita Moves Up

Several months later, Judi Rockwell called Savita into her office. "Savita, you have been doing a fine job. All the patients love you. You get your work done in a fast and friendly way. You have taken on extra work and have done it well. I think it is time to give you a raise," said Ms. Rockwell.

Savita smiled happily and told Ms. Rockwell about her plans to go to college. "The raise will help me pay for classes."

"I think we can help you with that, too. Since your college classes will help your work, the nursing home will pay for some of your classes," said Ms. Rockwell.

"I can't believe my luck!" said Savita.

"Oh, it's more than luck, Savita. It's hard work and the right attitude that helped you. I am glad you have joined our staff. If we can help you with your plans to go on to college, stop in and see me anytime," Judi Rockwell said, smiling at Savita.

Words, Words, Words

A. Some words have many meanings, depending on how they are used in a sentence. Read the sentences below. They come from the story. Put a √ next to the meaning of the underlined word in each sentence.

1. "I love to cook and <u>serve</u> food."

   a. _____ to hand over   b. _____ to hit a tennis ball

2. "I used to cook her favorite <u>dishes</u> and serve them to her."

   a. _____ plates to eat from

   b. _____ different types of food to serve

3. "You'll also need some uniforms, and you will need to get a physical <u>exam</u>."

   a. _____ a school test   b. _____ a checkup by a doctor

4. Finally, someone came through the food <u>line.</u>

   a. _____ a mark drawn on paper

   b. _____ a way people stand while waiting

5. "Savita, you have been doing a <u>fine</u> job."

   a. _____ a bill charged for breaking the law

   b. _____ good

B. Antonyms are words with opposite meanings. Synonyms are words with similar meanings. Read each pair of words below. Write **A** for antonym or **S** for synonym.

1. excited _____ bored

2. customer _____ buyer

Word Story:

You can arrange to have your paycheck directly deposited into the bank by your employer. Direct deposit *means part or all of your check goes into your checking or savings account. You do not have to go to the bank to deposit your check.*

3. cafeteria _____ lunchroom

4. uniform _____ work clothes

5. carefully _____ carelessly

C. Sometimes the vowels **ea** together can have the **long e sound.** Read the words below. They all have the vowels **ea** in them. Put a √ next to the words with a **long e sound.**

1. _____ app<u>ea</u>rance   2. _____ pl<u>ea</u>sed   3. _____ br<u>ea</u>d

4. _____ b<u>ea</u>d   5. _____ h<u>ea</u>d   6. _____ b<u>ea</u>rd

D. Sometimes the letters **ck** can sound like the letter **k.** Read the sentences below. Fill in the correct **ck** word to complete each sentence. Use the words in the list.

sucked   truck   tucked   duck   luck   stuck

1. Savita had good _____ finding a job.

2. Mika drives a _____ to bring food supplies to a restaurant.

3. Toru has a _____ for a pet.

4. The little boy made a face after he _____ on the lemon.

5. He _____ his shirt into his pants.

6. The car was _____ in the deep snow.

E. The suffix **-er** can mean *more* when added to a word.
   He is smaller than his brother.

The suffix **-est** can mean *most* when added to a word.
   He is the smallest child in class.

Add **-er** or **-est** to the words below. Use the new word in a sentence.

1. old + er _____

   _____

2. old + est _____

   _____

3. fast + er _____

   _____

Understanding

A. Read the sentences below. Use the story to help you.

1. Write some ways Savita helped her aging grandmother.

   _____

   _____

   _____

   _____

2. Write two things Savita did to make sure she was dressed correctly for her interview.

   _____

   _____

3. Write two things Savita's supervisor did to train her for her job.

   _____

   _____

B. A **fact** is something you know is true. An **opinion** is something you feel or believe. Read each sentence below. Write **F** for a fact. Write **O** for an opinion.

1. _____ Savita got a job as a food service worker.

2. _____ The interviewer thought Savita could do a good job.

3. _____ Savita was friendly to the nursing home patients.

4. _____ The first patient in Savita's line was nice.

5. _____ Savita's friendly smile was good for the patients.

Discussion

A. Put a √ next to your answer. Use the story to help you.

1. What is the **main idea** in the part called "Getting Ready for the Interview"?

   a. _____ Savita decides to go on a job interview.

   b. _____ Savita decides what to do after the interview.

   c. _____ Savita decides what to wear at the interview.

   d. _____ Savita decides how to get to the interview.

2. What is the **main idea** in the part called "Job Training"?

   a. _____ Savita trains her supervisor for the new job.

   b. _____ The supervisor trains Savita for her new job.

   c. _____ Savita learns the names of the patients.

   d. _____ Savita likes working with food and serving food.

B. A **cause** is what makes something happen. An **effect** is what happens. Write **C** next to the cause. Write **E** next to the effect.

1. _____ Savita met the requirements for the job.

   _____ Judi Rockwell asked Savita to fill out an application.

2. _____ Savita was hired as a food service worker.

   _____ Judi Rockwell liked the way Savita answered the interview questions.

3. _____ Savita did a fine job and had a good attitude.

   _____ Savita received a raise.

A Closer Look at Moving Up

WORKPLACE SKILLS

Finding a job is a big step that takes time and hard work. Once you get a job, you may think you can stop working so hard. But, did you know that the same hard work and skills you used to get your job are still important? Just because you have a job doesn't mean that you might not one day want to change jobs to get a better job.

Someday you may want to *move up the career ladder.* You may like the job you have, but you may feel you are capable of doing more. You may want to add to your present job by taking on more important tasks. You may also want to earn a higher salary.

Your Job Power Pyramid

To move up to the next level in a job, you need certain skills and knowledge about your current job as well as the job you want to do. You need the education to meet the demands of the job. This could be a high school diploma, a GED, a 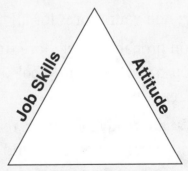 college degree, or some special training. You also need a positive attitude—an attitude that says "I know I can do it!" An attitude of friendliness, cooperation, and helpfulness is also important.

Following is a "test" to help you decide if you are ready to move up.

Check Yourself: Rate the following sentences as they apply to you.

Give yourself 1 point if the sentence is not often true about you.

Give yourself 2 points if the sentence is sometimes true about you.

Give yourself 3 points if the sentence is almost always true about you.

Job Skills

_____ I have a skill or skills that can be useful in my chosen work.

_____ I know I am as good as most others at the job I do.

_____ I make an effort to develop new job skills on a regular basis.

Education

_____ I have the necessary amount of education for the job I do.

_____ My life skills, which are the things I learned on my own like being responsible, managing my time, etc., help me on the job.

_____ I seek out more training whenever possible.

Attitude

_____ I am confident about my job skills and the way I do my job.

_____ I see myself in the future as being more successful than I am today.

_____ My personality is a plus, and it helps me on the job.

Scoring: Add your scores for all three areas. If your score is

9–15 You probably need more time to develop your potential before you try to move up. Look at your weak areas and try to strengthen them.

15-21 You are ready, or almost ready, to move up. Continue to address your weaknesses and build on your strengths. Be on the lookout for new jobs or job training that might be right for you.

21-27 You're ready to move up! Decide how you want to change or improve the job you have now. Then go after your goal.

Writing a Journal

Many people keep journals. They write about the things that happen to them each day. They tell about the people in their lives. They write about their feelings, joys, and sorrows. They write about their most private thoughts.

In Joan W. Blos's novel, *A Gathering of Days: A New England Girl's Journal, 1830–32,* you can read a journal that was kept by Catherine Hall.

Catherine wrote her journal during the last year she lived on the family farm. It tells the story about her daily life in a small New Hampshire town.

The following pages are selections from *A Gathering of Days.* Notice that each journal page has a date. The first page is dated November 20, 1899. That date is over 60 years after the journal was first started. It is a letter from Catherine Hall, the journal's writer, to her great-grandchild. In the letter, she explains to her great-granddaughter what the journal is about.

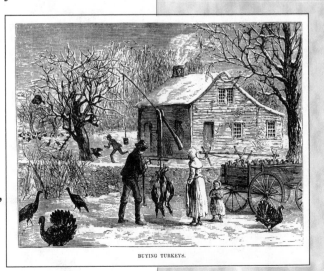

BUYING TURKEYS.

Read the next pages. Read the letter to find out about Catherine, her father, and her friend, Cassie. When you finish this selection, you may wish to go to the library to get the complete copy of *A Gathering of Days* to read.

The Reading Corner

Providence Rhode Island
November 20, 1899

To my namesake, Catherine:

I give you this book on your fourteenth birthday, as I turned fourteen the year of the journal; the year that was also my last on the farm tho' I did not know it then. It was also the year that my father remarried, and my best friend, Cassie, died. Cassie lives in my memory still, of all of us the only one never to grow old.

Once I might have wished for that: never to grow old. But now I know that to stay young always is also not to change. And that is what life's all about—changes going on every minute, and you never know when something begins where it's going to take you.

So one thing I want to say about life is don't be scared and don't hang back, and most of all, don't waste it.

Your loving great-grandmother,
Catherine Hall Onesti

Sunday, October 17, 1830

I, Catherine Cabot Hall, aged 13 years, 7 months, 8 days, of Meredith in the State of New-Hampshire, do begin this book.

It was given to me yesterday, my father returning from Boston, Massachusetts, where he had gone to obtain provisions for the months ahead.

My father's name is Charles: Charles Hall. I am daughter also of Hannah Cabot Hall, dead of a fever these four long years; and older sister to Mary Martha whose dark, curling hair resembles our mother's, but I have our mother's blue eyes.

My dearest friend is Cassie. The Shipman's farm lies *South* of ours, and is rather larger. Cassie is older than I by a year, but the same in height. We tell each other every thing; and each of us in the other's dear heart finds secret dreams reflected. Cassie's brothers are: David Horatio, older by a full two years; Asa Hale, my age exactly; and William Mason, the youngest. He is but a baby and called by every one "Willie."

This day being the Sabbath we attended services both morning and afternoon.

The Reading Corner

Tuesday, October 19, 1830

This be the precept the teacher set out today:
. . . let thy words be plain and true to the thoughts of thy heart.

These be the thoughts of my heart; that I may remain here for ever and ever; here in this house which my father has built with the labour of his two hands;

that no harm come to those I love: Father and my sister, Matty; Cassie, and the Shipman family; and Father's brother, our Uncle Jack; who mills when he needs money, and never took a wife;

also that I may train myself to want to do what I am asked to do;

last, and most bitter of all to confess, I wish that my hair were curly, as Matty's is, and our mother's.

Friday, October 22, 1830

We had a visitor today but nearly failed to admit him. No callers, surely, were expected. And peddlars, tinkers, and the like will not come by till Spring. Thus we ignored the rattling latch—at times the wind will mislead us so— until a voice called out.

It proved to be our Uncle Jack and tho' he protested he was just passing by, I thought he meant to visit. He brought some store sweets, wrapped in paper, and consented to have some cyder.

Tuesday, November 23, 1830

As the snow continued we did not go to school. Later, when it had abated, I cleared the pathway to the barn as a help to Father. It is quite uncommon to have snow so deep so early.

Monday, January 3, 1831

Teacher Holt, in school today, read from the *newspaper!*

Friday, January 7, 1831

Cassie, Asa, Matty, and I walked home from school together. He loudly lamented the great injustice that he must struggle with Arithmetic while Cassie and I, indeed all we girls, are excused by reason of our Sex from all but the simplest cyphering, and the first four rules.

We hoped to go sledding after. But Mr. Shipman had need of Asa, and too soon it was dark.

Tuesday, April 5, 1831

Scarcely a dozen of good apples left, and fewer still of cabbage! The larger potatoes are sprouting again! However, as this is the third time around, it will be the last time if I catch them quick enough. Parsnips, of course, are now at their best. I use them often, mashed and plain, or cook them into soup.

Wednesday, August 10, 1831

The dark-striped tabby had four kittens today and each of them a darling! We knew her time was nearly here, but had not thought so soon.

Cassie likes the pure white one best. I prefer the little black, whose two front paws are tipped.

They are too tiny to take in our hands, and sleep so curled and sweet.

The Reading Corner

Words, Words, Words

A. Read the sentences below. They are from Catherine Hall's journal. Put a √ next to the meaning of each underlined word.

1. It was given to me yesterday, my father returning from Boston, Massachusetts, where he had gone to obtain <u>provisions</u> for the months ahead.

   a. _____ food   b. _____ something that is provided

2. . . . and older sister to Mary Martha whose dark, curling hair <u>resembles</u> our mother's. . . .

   a. _____ similar to   b. _____ different from

3. He loudly lamented the great injustice that he must <u>struggle</u> with Arithmetic. . . .

   a. _____ push and shove   b. _____ make a strong effort

4. As the snow continued we did not go to school. Later, when it had <u>abated,</u> I cleared the pathway to the barn as a help to Father.

   a. _____ continued   b. _____ stopped

5. It is quite <u>uncommon</u> to have snow so deep so early.

   a. _____ usual   b. _____ unusual

B. A word to which a prefix or suffix can be added is a **base word.** Read the words below. Write the base words on the lines.

1. wished _____

2. going _____

3. older _____

4. nearly _____

5. uncommon _____

Understanding

A. Use the journal to help you answer the questions below.

1. What state did Catherine Hall live in? _____

2. What year did she begin her journal? _____

3. To whom did Catherine Hall leave her journal? _____

4. Who was Cassie? _____

5. What did Uncle Jack do when he needed money? _____

6. Who was Catherine's teacher? _____

7. What do you think "cyphering" means? _____

B. Write your answers on the line.

1. In the journal entry of Friday, January 7, 1831, Catherine writes, ". . . all we girls, are excused by reason of our Sex from all but the simplest cyphering, and the first four rules." What do you think she means by this entry? _____

   _____

2. In Catherine's letter to her great-granddaughter, she writes, "Cassie lives in my memory still, of all of us the only one never to grow old." What does Catherine mean by these words? Why didn't Cassie grow old? _____

   _____

   _____

   _____

   _____

You Can
Write a Journal

On the lines below, try to keep a journal for a few days. Use the style that Catherine used in her journal. Write the day and the date. Try to write every day. Put aside the same time each day. Pick a time that is convenient for you. You don't have to write a lot—maybe only a word or one sentence.

Date: _____

_____

_____

_____

_____

_____

_____

_____

_____

_____

_____

Date: _____

_____

_____

_____

_____

_____

_____

_____

_____

_____

_____

_____

_____

_____

_____

_____

_____

_____

_____

_____

_____

_____

_____

_____

_____

_____

A. Put a √ next to the synonym for the first word.

1. nervous   a. _____ carefree   b. _____ anxious

2. awake   a. _____ alert   b. _____ asleep

B. Put a √ next to the antonym for the first word.

3. bored   a. _____ quiet   b. _____ interesting

4. sweet   a. _____ sour   b. _____ good tasting

C. Put a √ next to the word that shows more than the first word in each row.

5. boy   a. _____ boys   b. _____ boyes

6. fox   a. _____ foxs   b. _____ foxes

7. gas   a. _____ gass   b. _____ gases

D. Put a √ next to the word that has a **k sound** for the letters **ch**.

8. a. _____ character   b. _____ such

9. a. _____ machine   b. _____ school

10. a. _____ chorus   b. _____ chili

E. Put a √ next to the two words in each row that have the same long vowel sound.

11. a. _____ vow   b. _____ rough   c. _____ pouch

12. a. _____ crow   b. _____ mouse   c. _____ gown

F. Make the following words show ownership.

13. the car that belongs to the parent

_____

14. the hats that belong to the girls

_____

G. Put a √ next to the meaning of the underlined word.

15. She <u>burst</u> through the door.

a. _____ broke   b. _____ rushed in

16. Grandmother Dombrick had trouble <u>hearing</u> her grandsons.

    a. _____ picking up voices   b. _____ court case

H. Read the story. Put a √ next to the best answer.

    I spent a year learning how to be a piano tuner. On my first day, I helped refinish a piano. It was very hard work. I sanded, sprayed, and sanded some more. I was very sore. But, I loved it!

    I also learned how to tune. Tuning is very difficult. I had to practice an hour every day. My ears got very tired. I also had to pull up each piano string. There are 230 strings in a piano. The work takes a lot of muscle.

    I started my own business in 1975. There were very few women tuners then. Many customers called and asked for my husband. They thought a woman could not be a piano tuner. I told them I was the tuner. Some said fine. Others hung up the phone.

    Today there are many women piano tuners. Tuners can work in homes, schools, churches, or piano factories.

17. What does *sore* mean in the first paragraph?

    a. _____ mad or angry

    b. _____ painful and tender

    c. _____ rise high in the air

18. How many strings are in a piano?

    a. _____ 1975   b. _____ 230   c. _____ 187

19. What does *Some said fine* mean in the next to last paragraph?

    a. _____ very small

    b. _____ the end in music

    c. _____ it's OK

20. People thought a woman could not be a tuner because

    a. _____ women were not smart enough.

    b. _____ it took a lot of muscle to pull the piano strings.

    c. _____ years ago some jobs were thought to be only a "man's job."

absence	time away from a place or an event	**diseases**	illnesses or sicknesses
absolutely	definitely, for sure	**embrace**	to hug
annoyance	something that bothers you	**environment**	surroundings
application	a form that contains information about you that you fill out in order to be interviewed for a job	**exact**	just right
		exam	a test
		fabulous	wonderful
aromas	smells or odors	**facility**	a building used for some activity or service
assumed	believed as true	**fibers**	roughage that helps you digest your food
attention	notice		
awkward	uncomfortable	**fixture**	something that is firmly in place like a door hinge, frying pan handle, or lightbulb socket
bicker	fight and quarrel		
bounded	leaped		
cancer masses	clumps of cancer cells	**grimly**	unsmilingly
chatted	talked happily	**hearing**	a legal interview
cleanliness	being clean, not dirty	**ignored**	failed to notice
clinics	places where people go to receive special care other than in a hospital or a nursing home	**image**	a mental idea or picture you have of yourself
		immunization	protection against disease or illness through shots
complained	found fault	**inoperable cancer**	cancer that has reached such a serious state that it cannot be removed through an operation
conservative	traditional, businesslike, not flashy or fancy		
contentedly	felt happy		
contributions	actions, things, or gifts given	**instances**	examples
cramped	close and crowded	**interrupt**	to stop
defensive	protective	**interrupted**	stopped
delicious	tastes very good	**interviewer**	a person who asks questions of someone trying to get a job
delighted	very happy		
dietary technicians	people who do a special job, usually helping a nutritionist	**job training**	teaching that shows how to do a certain job
		maintenance	keeping building, machines, cars in good condition
dietician	a nutritionist who has had four years of college and can work with special food needs for people in hospitals and nursing homes	**mammogram**	a medical test in which the breast is viewed by X ray
		murmur	soft noise
disability	physical problem		

nervous	unsure or uneasy	**reasonable**	showing good thinking
nutrition	healthy foods	**rehearsed**	repeated or practiced something over and over
nutritionist	a person who studies about nutrition and helps other people to learn to eat healthy foods	**relieved**	free from worry
		reluctantly	not willing to do something
optometrist	a person who tests the eyes for vision disorders	**required**	needed
		responded	answered
overlooked	ignored or not noticed something	**responsibility**	your duty to do something
oversized	bigger than most	**sari**	the main clothing worn by women in Pakistan. It is a long piece of cotton, silk, or other fabric.
Pakistan	an independent country in South Asia on the Arabian Sea. The capital is Islamabad. Pakistan is about the size of the state of Texas.	**scholarship**	a grant of money for schooling
		seldom	only once in a while
patients	people who are receiving care in a hospital or a nursing home	**site**	location
		smirked	smiled slyly
paused	stopped for a short time	**smugly**	with self-satisfaction
pertained	related to	**spices**	flavorings
possibility	can be done	**squinted**	closed one's eyes part way
prepared	made ready	**stoop**	small porch and steps in front of an apartment building or house
privacy	a place or situation in which a person is out of public view	**supervisor**	the person in charge; the boss
project	apartment buildings or houses	**swear**	to promise
promptly	in a short time; on time	**swelling**	to grow bigger and look like a lump
pronounce	to say	**sympathetically**	with understanding for another's feelings
protein	necessary parts in food for the body's growth	**trembling**	shaking
pudding	sweet dessert	**vaccinations**	another word for *immunization* or shots against certain diseases
rapidly	quickly	**verify**	to prove something is true
rarely	not often	**virus**	disease
reactions	responses		

Lesson 1

Words, Words, Words

A. 1. The blouse was shrunk before it was bought.   2. She wanted to move her students forward to the next grade.
3. Margo heated the oven before she put in the roast.   4. Republicans and Democrats favor democracy.   5. The airplane ticket must be paid for before the businessman could get it.

B. 2. thin, dry   3. huge, dangerous, mightily
4. thousand, tiny, sharp   5. hard, crying, red-faced

C. 2. frozen, cocoa   3. envelope, loan
4. slope, soak   5. blower, throat

D. 2. shadow   3. should, shield   4. shirtless,
shyly   5. shuffle, sharply

Understanding

A. 3. F   4. F   5. F   6. F   7. O

B. 1. Yes, she was used to living on her own; Yes, she will not want to be a burden any longer than she has to; Yes, that is her basic character. No, she might be afraid she'll hurt herself again.

2. She will have to be more careful; she will probably need to see a doctor more often; she will probably have to take more medicines; she might be afraid to live alone again; she might see her grandchildren more often.

3. No, they had to share a room. Yes, they loved their grandmother; not at first because the house got too crowded. But after they got used to that, they did.

4. No, because he won't have her help. Yes, because she helped him become more confident.

Discussion

A. 1. painted Micah's room, removed throw rugs, put a grab bar on the bath   2. she is 78 years old, she broke her hip, she lived alone for 15 years
Other possible answers: her daughter's name is Margo; her grandchildren love her;

she had to use a walker; sometimes she got cranky; she needed help getting dressed

B. 1. She fell and broke her hip.   2. Being cramped into one room.   3. His grandmother helped him study.   4. a. The boys watched less TV.   b. Margo was helped preparing dinner.

Lesson 2

Words, Words, Words

A. 2. ached   3. pronounce   4. scrubbing
5. kettle   6. applied   7. verify   8. swear
9. several

B. 1. b   2. a   3. b   4. a   5. b

C. 1. I knew the answer.   2. I had a knot in the shoestring.   3. He hurt his knee.
4. She knit a sweater.

D. 2, 3, 5, 6, 8.   10. I broke the teapot.   11. She is a nice landlady.   12. She knew herself very well.   13. The child rode his tricycle on the sidewalk.   14. He bought a new textbook.

Understanding

1. She will be able to vote. She will be eligible for U. S. citizen benefits.   2. She would take the test again until she passed.
3. Yes, voting is important. No, she could have talked about her family and its needs.
4. There are many people trying to get U. S. citizenship.

Discussion

A. a. 5   b. 7   c. 1   d. 3   e. 6   f. 2   g. 4

B. 1. at the business tower   2. Form N-400
3. INS office   4. 1 boy   5. 18 years old
6. Mrs. Forello   7. Ms. Allen   8. She wanted to vote.   9. She wanted to tell her son and friends.

A Closer Look at Test Taking

I would review, join a study group, and get a good night's rest before the test.

Lesson 3

Words, Words, Words

A. 1. b 2. a 3. b 4. c
B. 1. b 2. b 3. b 4. c
C. 3. hawk's beak 4. turkeys' voices 5. fox's den
   6. father's name 7. girls' teams
D. 2. ugly 3. family 4. any 5. Lucy
E. 1. squint 2. squeeze 3. squash 4. squeal
   5. squirm

Understanding

A. 1. Carly's mom was comfortable with her. She spent time with her. Carly's dad ignored her. He didn't spend time with her.
   2. They both spent time doing things with her.
B. 1. b 2. c 3. b

Discussion

A. a. 2 b. 1 c. 4 d. 3
B. 2. Cause: rain Effect: flowers grew
   3. Cause: Mary put on her jacket. Effect: She felt warmer.
   4. Cause: Jack fell off the ladder. Effect: He broke his leg.

Lesson 4

Words, Words, Words

A. 1. b 2. a 3. b 4. b
B. 1. talker She is a constant talker. 2. respectful She answered in a respectful way. or respectable He lives in a respectable community. 3. truthful He is truthful. 4. management He works in management.
C. 2. spy 3. reply 4. sly 5. buy 6. sky 7. apply
D. 2, 3, 4, 6, 7

Understanding

A. 1. Elisa didn't want to wear glasses. 2. Her parents wanted her to wear the glasses because Elisa needed them to see.
B. 1. Yes, I would be patient with my child and try to make him or her feel better about the glasses. I would explain the need for them and assure the child it would not ruin the way he or she looks. 2. I would get the glasses if I could afford them. I would try to find a way to get the glasses. 3. I would not like the thought at first but would eventually get used to it.

Discussion

A. 1. Elisa squinted and watched TV very close.
   2. She had trouble looking at the board, but worked OK at her desk. 3. You can see things well close but not far away. 4. Other people had bought glasses from him and were happy with his work.
B. 1. Elisa had trouble seeing in school and at home. 2. Joan talked to the teacher. 3. Elisa saw the school nurse. 4. Joan and Miguel took Elisa to the eye doctor. 5. Elisa told her friends she would need glasses.

You Can Solve the Problem

1. Stop and think, take a deep breath, don't do or say something he would regret.
2. I am scared that I may lose the love of my children. I am scared my children won't like their new stepfather or he won't like them.
3. I will let my children know I love them and their mother loves them.
4. Yell at ex-wife, bad-mouth new stepfather, explain situation to kids, assure kids that you love them, spend more time with kids, get to know new stepfather, help kids figure out what to call new stepfather.
5. Yell at ex-wife, wouldn't solve problem, could hurt kids/ex-wife, won't get you closer to your goal. Bad-mouth new stepfather, wouldn't solve problem, won't get you closer to your goal, could hurt kids/ex-wife/new stepfather.
6. Keep in mind the goal he chose.
7. Choice must meet goal in Step 3—"I will let my children know I love them."

Lesson 5

Words, Words, Words

A. 2. endless 3. shameful 4. strapless 5. glassful
   6. joyless
B. 2. changing lightbulbs 3. hear 4. wrench
   5. customers
C. 3. blouse, eyebrow 4. mouse, gown 5. crouch, frown 6. ground, growl 7. vow, pouch
D. 3, 5, 6, 7, 9 1. The snow made a pretty scene.
   2. The dog picked up the rabbit's scent.
   3. Science is my favorite subject.

Understanding

A. 1. He was up long before dawn. 2. They both wanted to make good impressions on someone who could help them achieve something; They both made lists of their accomplishments and future plans to present to the individual who could help them.

B. 1. He might want a raise so that he could afford improvements in his home or lifestyle, such as buying a car, new clothes, or going on a vacation; so that he could raise a family; so that he could save toward retirement.   2. Mr. Kennedy will be successful in getting Anthony a raise because he has a good case; He will not get Anthony's raise because there is not enough money in the hotel's budget; He will get the raise for Anthony, but not for a while.   3. No, because he has not shown much concern for Anthony's financial well-being in the past; No, because as a boss he is more interested in saving the company money; Yes, because he likes Anthony and has even complimented him; Yes, because there is probably a hotel rule about giving raises.

Discussion
A. a. 2   b. 1   c. 3   d. 4
B. 1. c   2. c   3. d

You Can Follow Directions
1. No, the shirt shrunk because it should be washed in warm water not hot water.   2. warm   3. yes   4. Color can transfer onto your skin or other materials like a sweater worn over the shirt.   5. He washed it in hot water.   6. yes, but only non-chlorine bleach   7. remove promptly   8. No, he caused the shirt to shrink by not following the care directions.   9. inside collar or side label   10. Give it away.

Lesson 6
Words, Words, Words
A. 2. bound   3. call   4. look   5. tell   6. smug   7. annoy   8. whisper   9. play   10. respond
B. 1. a. doorway   b. hallway   c. understanding or forgot   3. day light   I see better in daylight.   4. meat loaf   We had meatloaf for dinner.   5. make up   She wore eye makeup.
C. 1. soap   2. cloak   3. throat   4. groan   5. soak   6. cocoa
D. 4, 8   10. I like school.
E. 4. rules   5. glasses   6. aromas   7. messages   8. bosses   9. illnesses   10. sisters

Understanding
A. 1. O   2. F   3. F   4. F   5. F
B. 1. b   2. a   3. b   4. b   5. a

Discussion
A. take messages; use a greeting; ask the caller's name; use 911 for emergencies; write down day and time of call
B. a. 6   b. 1   c. 5   d. 4   e. 2   f. 3
C. Maybe someday when they can afford it.

A Closer Look at Becoming a Voter
A. 1. 23   2. Last name   3. Answers will vary.   4. 8/15/98   5. Croatia   6. Answers will vary.   7. No   8. a. No   b. Answers will vary.   9. 3 signatures/1 printed   10. To help verify the person's identity   11. What county do you live in?   12. Answers will vary.   13. She would print her name—Neda Kolich.   14. I would print my name.   15. If someone helped the applicant fill out this form, he or she would have to give his or her name.

Lesson 7
Words, Words, Words
A. 1. b   2. a   3. a
B. 1. the doctor's office   2. Mrs. Kyle's purse   3. Chester's notebook   4. the doctor's arm   5. Mrs. Kyle's shoe
C. 1. churches   2. diseases   3. problems   4. brushes   5. beaches   6. diets   7. shots   8. birches
D. 1. soar/four   2. fruit/loot   3. fool/school   4. rear/deer
E. 1. childhood   2. Chester   3. chart   4. children   5. choking   6. catch   7. child   8. checkup

Understanding
A. 1. Differences: Measles cause a cough and a rash and possible brain damage; mumps cause headache and swelling of the jaw.
    Same: They both cause fever and possible hearing loss and are easily passed from one person to another.
    2. Same: The DTP vaccination protects against these diseases.
    Differences: People can die from diphtheria; pertussis can cause brain damage.
B. 1. b   2. c   3. a

Discussion
A. 1. diphtheria, tetanus, and pertussis   2. German measles   3. a person is unable to walk or move; breathing problems   4. Side effects are: loss of energy, site of the shot is sore, low fever

B. 2. Cause: rubella caught by women in the early stages of pregnancy; Effect: loss of fetus or birth defects
   3. Cause: HIB disease; Effect: brain damage

Lesson 8

Words, Words, Words

A. 2. a letter   3. the letter   4. jewelry box
   5. mammograms
B. 2. b   3. a   4. b
C. 1. pound/sound   2. couple/trouble   3. house/loud
   4. spouse/plough   5. couch/pouch
D. 1. k   2. s   3. k   4. k   5. k   6. s   7. k   8. k, s
   9. k, s   10. k
E. 1. gases   2. partners   3. classes   4. letters
   5. adults

Understanding

A. 1. F   2. F   3. F   4. F   5. O   6. O   7. F   8. O
   9. F   10. O
B. 1. a lump in the breast   2. nipple discharge
   3. change in shape or color of breast

Discussion

A. 1. c   2. b   3. b
B. 1. C/E   2. E/C

A Closer Look at Food Labels

A. 1. A, C   2. 0 mg   3. Yes, the label says so.
   4. water   5. No, it only has 1 g.   6. Yes, it has 0 g
   of fat and saturated fat   7. Yes, because it
   provides vitamins;   No, it doesn't have enough
   vitamins.   8. Yes, fresh fruits are more
   nutritious.   9. cottage cheese or other fruits or
   gelatin   10. China

Lesson 9

Words, Words, Words

A. 1. b   2. c   3. a
B. 1. c   2. b   3. c
C. 1. wrinkled   2. wrist, wreck   3. wrestling
   4. wreath
D. 1. windshield   The car windshield had ice on it.
   2. bookshelf   The bookshelf is new.
   3. humankind   Humankind is another word for
      mankind.
   4. necklace   She got a necklace for her birthday.
   5. earthquake   He read about the earthquake.
   6. milkshake   I drank a vanilla milkshake.
E. 1. worked   I worked last night.
   2. enjoyed   He enjoyed the play.

3. chewed   He chewed the meat slowly.
   4. learned   He learned the song.
   5. wanted   I wanted the new dress.
F. 1. foxes   2. fingers   3. fibers   4. taxes
   5. vitamins   6. sixes

Understanding

A. 2. She knew it would be a good example for the
   children.   3. These were fruits from her
   homeland.   4. The children could eat them
   easily.   5. They wanted to share with the
   children something from their homeland of
   Pakistan.
B. Yes, it is easy to eat and is healthy; No, children
   like icing cakes.   2. fruits and vegetables can be
   fun to eat; people from other countries have
   shared many new foods with the United States.

Discussion

A. 1. Cause: the icing was flavored; Effect: it tasted
   good   2. Cause: needed appealing finger food;
   Effect: cut the celery into small pieces
   3. Cause: honey was in the pudding; Effect:
   pudding was sweet
B. 1. Mara wanted to help people grow strong and
   fight disease.   2. Tashi wants her mother to help
   people grow strong and healthy.

You Can Tell What's Happening

B. 1. at home   2. two people   3. The father is
   giving some medicine to his son.
C. Answers will vary.

Lesson 10

Words, Words, Words

A. 2. parents   3. hot dogs, hamburgers, nachos,
   french fries   4. people   5. nutritionists
B. 1. restaurant's food   2. food service worker's job
   3. families' meals   4. hospitals' helpers
   5. cafeteria's trays
C. cry: try, my, buy, why; lady: healthy, hurry,
   dietary, every
D. 1, 4, 9, 11, 15, 18

Understanding

A. 1. They are too busy; They eat fast food.   2. Fast
   foods are higher in fat and lower in nutrition
   than foods made at home.   3. Go back to school;
   find a job where she or he could be trained on
   the job.
B. Yes, it gives you a chance to talk and share; No,
   people are used to eating fast food and like it.

Discussion
A. 1. vitamins and low fats   2. nutritionists
   3. nutritionist, dietary technician, food service
   worker
B. 1. a   2. b

Lesson 11
Words, Words, Words
A. 1. a   2. b   3. b   4. b   5. b
B. 1. A   2. S   3. S   4. S   5. A
C. 2, 4
D. 1. luck   2. truck   3. duck   4. sucked   5. tucked
   6. stuck
E. 1. He is older than Sam.   2. She is the oldest
   child.   3. This is a faster car.

Understanding
A. 1. She cooked her favorite foods and served them
   to her.   2. She put on a conservative dress; She
   made sure her hair and makeup were neat and
   clean.   3. He showed her how much food to put
   on the plates; He showed her how to set the
   cooked foods on the service line.
B. 1. F   2. F   3. F   4. F   5. O

Discussion
A. 1. c   2. b
B. 1. C/E   2. E/C   3. C/E

A Closer Look at Moving Up
Answers will vary.

The Reading Corner
Words, Words, Words
A. 1. a   2. a   3. b   4. b   5. b
B. 1. wish   2. go   3. old   4. near   5. common

Understanding
A. 1. New Hampshire   2. 1830   3. her great-
   granddaughter   4. Catherine's best friend
   5. he mills   6. Teacher Holt   7. working with
   numbers *or* doing arithmetic
B. 1. In those days, girls were expected to get
   married and have children; girls were thought
   not to be as smart as men so they wouldn't
   understand arithmetic.
   2. Cassie died and never had a chance to grow
   old. Catherine's memories of Cassie are only
   those of Cassie as a child.